Kingdom Centric
Reframing Christianity

Paul Clayton Gibbs

Kingdom Centric: Reframing Christianity
Copyright © 2024 by Paul Clayton Gibbs

Published by Harris House Publishing
harrishousepublishing.com
Arlington, Texas
USA

This title is available in other formats.
ISBN: 978-1-946369-64-2

Cover creation by Jodeci Dunick | design by Paul Clayton Gibbs

All Scripture quotations, unless otherwise indicated, are taken from the Holy Bible, New International Version®, NIV®. Copyright ©1973, 1978, 1984, 2011 by Biblica, Inc.® Used by permission of Zondervan. All rights reserved worldwide. www.zondervan.com The "NIV" and "New International Version" are trademarks registered in the United States Patent and Trademark Office by Biblica, Inc.®

Scripture quotations marked (NLT) are taken from the Holy Bible, New Living Translation, copyright ©1996, 2004, 2015 by Tyndale House Foundation. Used by permission of Tyndale House Publishers, Carol Stream, Illinois 60188. All rights reserved.

Scripture quotations marked ESV are from the ESV® Bible (The Holy Bible, English Standard Version®), © 2001 by Crossway, a publishing ministry of Good News Publishers. Used by permission. All rights reserved. The ESV text may not be quoted in any publication made available to the public by a Creative Commons license. The ESV may not be translated in whole or in part into any other language.

Scripture quotations marked NKJV are taken from the New King James Version®. Copyright © 1982 by Thomas Nelson. Used by permission. All rights reserved.

Scripture quotations marked MEV are taken from the Modern English Version. Copyright © 2014 by Military Bible Association. Used by permission. All rights reserved.

Scripture quotations marked MSG are taken from The Message, copyright © 1993, 2002, 2018 by Eugene H. Peterson. Used by permission of NavPress. All rights reserved. Represented by Tyndale House Publishers.

Scripture quotations from The Authorized (King James) Version. Rights in the Authorized Version in the United Kingdom are vested in the Crown. Reproduced by permission of the Crown's patentee, Cambridge University Press.

Scripture quotations marked CJB are taken from the Complete Jewish Bible by David H. Stern. Copyright © 1998. All rights reserved. Used by permission of Messianic Jewish Publishers, 6120 Day Long Lane, Clarksville, MD 21029. www.messianicjewish.net.

Scripture quotations marked NRSVUE are taken from the New Revised Standard Version Updated Edition. Copyright © 2021 National Council of Churches of Christ in the United States of America. Used by permission. All rights reserved worldwide.

All rights reserved. No portion of this book may be reproduced, stored in a retrieval system, or transmitted in any form or by any means—electronic, mechanical, photocopy, recording, or any other—except for brief quotation in printed reviews, without the prior permission of the publisher.

Kingdom Centric™ items, feedback report, training curricula, and e-learning are the property of Masterclass Suites, LLC, 2024. All rights reserved.

www.ingramcontent.com/pod-product-compliance
Lightning Source LLC
Chambersburg PA
CBHW070144080526
44586CB00015B/1830

The Scalpel

This teaching, like a scalpel, cuts through the false logic that justifies consumerist Christianity. It wraps fresh answers in practical application, and you can't unsee the optimistic picture Gibbs paints of a life truly worth living. Such a challenging alternative to self-oriented Christianity!

Patrick Hegarty | Senior Pastor Kenmore Church | Australia

The Blueprint

What if you first have to unlearn before you learn? In this thought-provoking book, Gibbs provides us with a blueprint to reframe and re-think our well-established paradigms, thus enabling us to return to God's original design for our lives and our churches.

Paul Bartlett | ACC State President | Australia

The Motivator

This book is a must-read! It motivates me to focus more on advancing God's Kingdom and less on my own preferences and ministries. I'm reading it a second time and becoming more 'Kingdom-Centric' both in my heart and in my head. Get your pen and highlighter; we have work to do!

Becca Landers | Worship Leader The Life Church | USA

The Challenge

If you have ever felt like there is more to this Christian journey, this book is for you. Once again, Gibbs's writing is challenging, scriptural, and, at times, hilarious. His pointed questions require contemplation, helping us redefine our relationship with God.

Carl Walker | Founder En Gedi Retreat | USA

The Insight

This book is an outstanding insight into the original roots of our faith and the Church. It moves us away from a Westernised form of faith to a Biblical and first-century modus operandi, enabling us to become nimble, vibrant, and focused on discipling nations.

Ian Green | President of Kingdomize Global | UK

The Pathway

Kingdom Centric provides a pathway to reformation our churches so desperately need. You cannot simply read it; it should be studied and understood, shared and actioned. It really is that important.

Carol Prater | Co-Pastor New Hope Church | Australia

The Choice
Gibbs presents a choice between the two models of Christianity and skilfully articulates them from the viewpoint of the kingdom of God. Heartsearching questions propel us to choose how we can also journey towards the Father.

Elaine Swinney | Parish Nurse | UK

The Logic
This book should be on every Christian's required reading. Written in the author's matter-of-fact style. It's an enjoyable read, and I found myself in complete agreement with the logic and direction of the Kingdom-Centric perspective. Definitely five-stars!

James Burgess | Aviation Technician | USA

The Guide
As a family man, embracing the Kingdom-Centric principles has guided me toward pursuing the husband and father I was created to be. Its tools have been instrumental in refocusing me on the desires in God's heart, not just the blessings in His hands!

Manuel Delgado | Marketing Consultant | Faroe Islands

The Groundbreaker
I really enjoy Gibbs's succinct writing, and this book delivers groundbreaking insights for those transitioning from being a mere receiver to an advancer of the Kingdom. I found the chapters on both Church and Calling especially affirming.

Michael Simmonds | Teacher | Denmark

The Heart-check
If you feel stuck, unfruitful, or worried you've missed the point, then this book will challenge you from a place of love, and without judgment. It's all about the heart. It's a must-read!

Sophie O'Connor | Premier League Football Systems Manager | UK

The Transformation
What would happen if we truly made God's Kingdom our primary concern? This thought-provoking teaching encourages us to embark on a spiritual transformation journey. One that will change us in such a way that the world will know we are truly disciples of Jesus.

Ruven Dominik | Global Financial Institution | Switzerland

To those who know we can do better.

Kingdom Centric

Reframing Christianity

01 | Religion   9

02 | Gospel   21

03 | Righteousness   35

04 | Bible   49

05 | Church   63

06 | Prayer   76

07 | Calling   89

08 | Serving   102

09 | Giving   115

10 | Discipleship   127

How Kingdom-centric are you? Take the test:

01 | Religion

Ligare

Seek

I became a Christian in a tent at the age of 13.

Born with eczema, I had lived with the irritating skin condition all my life, but it had become septic and painfully debilitating by the time I was a teenager. It was so bad that I had to soak in a bath when my bandages were replaced to keep my skin from peeling off. My mother, a nurse, had been told by specialists that the treatment to reduce the infection would take at least nine months. This meant lots of lotions, sun lamps, and the occasional bottle of Guinness, which she was convinced would be good for me.

At that time, a week-long 'tent crusade' was being advertised in the area, and a few teenage boys from my school attended each night. Like me, none of my fellow students were particularly religious, and yet every morning, they came into class sharing what they had experienced. They mocked the people they had seen singing hymns and raising their arms in worship, but they also reported strange stories of people being healed of various physical conditions. On the last day of the event, one schoolmate said,

"Paul, you should go, because you're a bit like a cripple!"

And so, I did. And so, it happened. For the first time in my life, I heard the Gospel. I did not fully understand it, but somehow I knew it was true. At the end of the message, I took the opportunity to respond by repeating a prayer. After this, the evangelist invited those who had prayed to put their hand in the air. I thought this was odd, but cautiously I raised my hand. He then asked those who had put their hand up to stand up. I decided to do this one last thing and no more. But then, he gave an even bigger request: "If you have stood up, would you please walk to the back of the stage where someone will share the next steps?"

No way! It was all getting a little too much for me.

Enough was enough.

However, just then, the cute blonde I had been watching during the service responded, and suddenly, I felt God 'call me' to go forward as well. It seems God does work in (not so) mysterious ways. Yet I hadn't realized that by going forward, I would miss out on the part of the service where the sick were healed. By the time I had finished giving my life to Jesus, the service had finished, and instead of receiving a healing prayer, I was invited to attend church, which again posed the question:

> Was I prepared to take that next step?

I was, and during the first youth service I attended, I heard yet another sermon about moving toward something that I did not fully understand:

> *"But seek ye first the kingdom of God, and his righteousness; and all these things shall be added unto you."*[1]

I was told I did not need a priest to intercede for me but that I could seek God by praying to Him directly. And so, that evening, I knelt by my bedside and asked Him to heal me. Nine days later, not only had the septic infection disappeared, but so had all my eczema! I have never suffered since.

I realized this was both good news and bad news.

The good news is that God is real, the Bible is true, and heaven is a reality. The bad news is that the devil is real, the Bible is true, and hell is a reality. I knew then that I had to tell people what I had experienced, that following Jesus was a matter of eternal life and death.

To 'follow Jesus' of course implies moving in a specific direction. The night I first believed followed a pattern that has continued throughout my Christian journey: God shows me just enough to take the next step, but there is always more to come. Something that is hidden at first. Something a little complicated, a little odd. A more significant challenge but with a greater outcome that can only be discovered *as long as I keep moving forward.*

But how do I know if the direction I am moving is the one Jesus had in mind?

Discovering God's vision for our lives happens mainly in an awkward conversation with God, which starts when He does something to get our attention and then asks us a difficult question. My eczema got my attention, but it was that first awkward question, *"Will you follow Jesus?"* that initially moved me in the right direction. As we keep asking Him awkward follow-up questions, and allow Him to ask them in return, His direction becomes more precise and refined over time. However, if we stop seeking new answers or listening to His questions, our vision can stagnate and His purposes may be lost.

This book is for those who want to keep moving forward!

It contains details of the most awkward conversation I have ever had with God. One that began with a question that took me completely by surprise and an answer that is changing me in ways I could never have imagined.

Today, I would like to invite you into that awkward conversation.

Disconnect

I will never forget how it started.

It was unexpected and a little confusing, and I initially dismissed it. I was in a meeting discussing a plan or opportunity with the leaders of one of the churches I had emigrated from England to serve. While admiring the modern conference room with its green-tinged windows and high-end furnishings, I leaned back into my soft reclining chair when my mind was suddenly overtaken by a question that had never occurred to me before . . .

   "Is this a different religion?"

Although the thought caught me entirely off guard, this wasn't the first time I felt like I did not quite 'fit in' when discussing the work of God with other Christians. Therefore, what came to mind wasn't so much directed at the people in the room but was the culmination of questions that had built up over time and were suddenly being brought into focus.

Have you ever felt a similar disconnect?

Surprisingly, no scholarly consensus exists regarding what constitutes a religion; historians have struggled to agree on the definition of the word.[2] So, for

the purpose of our conversation, I want to add mine. The origin of the word 'religion' lies in the Latin word *'ligare'* meaning 'to bind.' It is where we get the word *'ligament,'* a band of tissue that connects bones, joints, or organs. Because of this, I define religion as:

> 'The way we connect with God.'

Jesus had a problem with religion, but it's not what you think. He had issues with those who taught religion but not with religion itself. He criticized the Pharisees' motives for their religious leadership but told His disciples to follow their religious teaching.[3] He also convinced the crowds that He had not come to alter their religious law but to complete it.

> *"Do not think that I have come to abolish the Law or the Prophets; I have not come to abolish them but to fulfill them."* [4]

I understand why, as Christians, we can be embarrassed to be seen as religious. Religion can be divisive, and many an evil intent has used religion to get what it wants. Sadly, however, we seem driven to make peculiar statements such as:

"Christianity is not a *religion*; it's a *relationship*."

Well, no, I'm afraid it *is* a religion.

Perhaps it is better to say: *"Christianity does not feel like a religion but more like a relationship!"* Or something along those lines. The point is Jesus' concern wasn't that His followers were religious but that their religion was not directed toward *His intended purpose.*

It makes me ask: What is Jesus' intended purpose for our religion?

Something about the intention of the choices we were making in that church conference room confused me, but I could not put my finger on what it was. I had no doubt that everyone I collaborated with knew and loved Jesus very much. Yet many of the plans that were made felt odd to me, and I am presuming so many of mine felt strange to them. At times, our motives seemed out of sync. Occasionally, I was told the issue was that I was British and had yet to understand the American culture. I'm sure there were elements of truth to that; however, while we joked about the difference in our accents, sometimes, it felt like we were speaking two entirely different languages.

Then, one day, I began to figure out why.

Around that time, we bought our son an old Xbox, and the following thought went through my mind. What would happen if he discovered a fantastic game and took the disc to his friend, encouraging him to try it? His friend, the proud owner of a PlayStation (a similar looking but different machine), might load the disc and press play, but nothing would happen. And so, a little confused, he'd likely reject the game and hand it back to my son. If so, would the problem be with the game my son gave him?

No. The problem would be that they had two different operating systems.

Was that my situation? Was my religion based on a different operating system? Just as the two gaming machines read the disc differently, were we reading the message of Jesus differently? Were the differences in the decisions we were making a response to two different ways of connecting with God?

I think they were.

I have been through a spiritual transformation since becoming a Christian. The religion I had when I first believed is being replaced by a new understanding of what it means to follow Jesus, and that 'reframing' of my Christianity conflicts with the one I was experiencing at the time. In fact, I have only recently found the language to understand and communicate the two operating systems. So, before I unpack them, let me share that language with you.

My definition of the two religions pivots on what we are pursuing:

> Christian-centric: *We pursue our vision, God's way, so He gives us what we want.*
>
> Kingdom-centric: *We pursue God's Kingdom, God's way, so we give Him what He wants.*

The difference between these two perspectives will shape our relationship with God. Converting to a more Kingdom-centric life will dramatically impact how we engage with the Father and, importantly, how the Father will engage with us! Therefore, I am inviting you to reframe your Christianity by connecting with Him from an increasingly Kingdom-centric perspective. Before we

unpack how we can do that, however, it is essential to remember the following:

    Both of the Christianities are Christianity.

    Both lead us toward heaven.

    Both are founded on salvation through Jesus Christ.

Yet, one makes our religion, by all intents and purposes, about us, while the other directs us towards *His intended purpose* for our religion.

And so, here is my first awkward question for you:

    Which of the two *religions* are you following?

Firstly, let me stress that being more one or the other is not a matter of how much God loves us but how much we love God. I do not encourage you to be Kingdom-centric so that you might somehow win more of God's love but instead to better direct your love for Him.

Secondly, this is not a call to choose sides. It is not one versus the other but a call to go beyond one to the other. It is not that a Christian-centric religion is bad, but that we can do better!

Thirdly, we are neither Christian-centric *nor* Kingdom-centric but a percentage of both; therefore, this reframing of our religion is not intended to label us or create a box for us. Instead, it is to aid our ongoing pursuit of a relationship that pleases the Father, one that fulfills His purpose and reflects the kind of Christianity He wants.

God's work rarely happens instantaneously and must be 'worked through.'

> *". . . continue to work out your salvation with fear and trembling, for it is God who works in you to will and to act in order to fulfill his good purpose."*[5]

Therefore, in this book, I will address the various 'pivots' upon which you can assess how Christian or Kingdom-centric you are. In this way, I hope that together we can make the decisions that will move us toward God's true purpose for our religion because, as you will see, truth is key.

Jesus said:

> *"[A] time is coming and has now come when the true worshipers will worship the Father in Spirit and in truth, for they are the kinds of worshipers the Father seeks."* [6]

I find that quite shocking because Jesus was not referring to unbelievers, and therefore, He infers there is a kind of worshipper the Father is *not* looking for! The 'wrong kind' of the worshipper is somehow a 'kind' in the wrong way.

So, what might that look like, and what's the alternative?

Christian

Question: *When might we miss Jesus' point?*

Answer: *When we miss His context.*

Just like you, I am positively influenced by the actions and mindsets of my fellow believers, but not everything I hear and see aligns with what Jesus said and did.

Is that the same for you?

Over the years, I have felt some conflict between the Christianity I am taught and the one I read in the Bible. Therefore, I want to base my actions on those of Jesus rather than a second-hand version that I might see in others or a hand-me-down narrative of what I am told He meant. This has encouraged me to ask more questions about the context in which Jesus spoke, and as I have, I've realized that almost everything Christ said . . . He said to believers.

You don't find Jesus trying to convince non-believers there is a God.

He never points to the wind and tells them: *"You cannot see it, but you can feel its effects!"* or other apologetic gems we find helpful to use. Almost everyone He preached to already believed. Therefore, all the passages we use to communicate the Gospel to non-believers were initially spoken to teach believers something they had not yet understood about the *intended purpose* of their religion.

Interestingly, some of the most evangelistic scriptures Christians use to reach non-believers were spoken to Jesus' hardcore followers, those who were truly pursuing Him, those I will refer to as pilgrims.

His defining statement . . . *"I am the way and the truth and the life. No one comes to the Father except through me"*[7] . . .comes from a conversation, awkward at times, with His inner circle, including Thomas, Philip, and Judas.

The mantra of all evangelists and many sports fans . . . *"For God so loved the world that he gave his one and only Son, that whoever believes in him shall not perish but have eternal life"*[8] . . .was His response to a committed but confused Nicodemus, a devoted God-fearing Jew.

Similarly, the most profound statement Jesus made about the kind of worshipper He was looking for was to those so interested in what He had to say that they followed Him up a mountain to hear Him say it!

> *"So do not worry, saying, 'What shall we eat?' or 'What shall we drink?' or 'What shall we wear?' For the pagans run after all these things, and your heavenly Father knows that you need them. But seek first his kingdom and his righteousness, and all these things will be given to you as well."*[9]

It turns out that the answer to the question, *"Is this a different religion?"* was hidden within the first passage of scripture I learned in church. Significantly, in the Sermon on the Mount, Jesus highlighted the two different operating systems by comparing the religion of the Jews to that of the pagans.

So, who were these pagans?

For years, I believed they represented those who ignored God or godly things and sought fulfillment in worldly possessions. After all, Jesus said, *"For the pagans run after these things,"* therefore inferring that we should not. But did He simply mean we shouldn't seek fulfillment in worldly possessions? Or was He getting at something far more profound?

Both pagans and pilgrims were on a spiritual journey, but the religion of the pagans meant they would seek divine direction through a process of sacrifice and 'oracles.'[10] Their sacrifice would allow them to ask their gods for direction and blessing for their lives. They might be considering a career change:

> "Would Apollo tell me if he would bless me in this venture?"

Or maybe, as in one famous case, the request would concern a military campaign:

"Should I go to war, and if I do, will the gods grant me victory?"

The answers could be ambiguous. In the case of Croesus, King of Lydia, who was considering going to war with Persia, he asked Apollo's oracle whether or not he would be victorious. Eventually, he was given the reply . . .

"A nation will fall."[11]

Which, as you can imagine, was not particularly helpful.

So, was Jesus' point that the pagans spent a lot of time, energy, and effort to get one ambiguous word from their god, while the Jews had an entire book full of wisdom they could look to? No. Those He spoke to already understood that! Instead, Jesus's concern was that the Jews' purpose appeared no different from that of the pagans; they were seeking everything the rest of the world wanted but believed that their God was the one who could get it for them!

Jesus was pointing out that what should separate the pilgrims from the pagans were the questions they asked:

Pagan: "Lord, if I do this, will You bless me?"

Pilgrim: "Lord, what are You doing, and how can I bless You?"

Pagans used their gods to seek worldly things, and to be Christian-centric is to do the same. It means seeking everything the world seeks but following the Father because, in doing so, we believe He will give it to us. Conversely, to be Kingdom-centric is to prioritize what God desires so that we can fulfill His purposes.

So, what about you? Which of the two Christianities best describes your connection with God? Is the primary intention of your religion to give Him what He wants or to get from Him what you believe He wants to give you?

A bit of both?

By comparing His pilgrims to the pagans, Jesus highlighted that there have always been two ways to follow God, and perhaps there always will be. They pre-date Protestantism and Catholicism, Arminianism and Calvinism, Dispensationalism and Covenantalism; they pre-date most *isms*. The two versions of Judaism, the one Jesus *witnessed* and the one Jesus *wanted*,

eventually led to two different Christianities. So, where are you on your journey, and how might you move forward?

Kingdom

Question: *How do we move forward?*

Answer: *One step at a time.*

Becoming Kingdom-centric is not a one-time decision.

It is like giving a $100 bill to God. We hand over the note, and He passes it right back to us in 10,000 cents. Occasionally, He will ask us for one of the pennies we had already dedicated to Him. Every request for a penny represents a choice. It is an opportunity—not to consider *if* we should give it but to reconsider *why* we are giving it!

On that journey of 10,000 pennies, I've begun to understand the following:

First, it's an ongoing *process*.

Jesus did not instantly fix the problem. Sadly, the 'Jew-Centric' form of Judaism had already morphed into the 'Christian-centric' form of Christianity when Paul wrote to the saints in Philippi:

> *"For everyone looks out for their own interests, not those of Jesus Christ."*[12]

The issue is still seen in all of Christendom, and the Christian-centric form of Christianity has been gathering speed. There is now an endless list of Christian books, podcasts, and blogs that promote pursuing our vision, God's way, so He gives us what we want. The more extreme versions focus on living our best lives now and imply that Jesus' sole purpose is to improve our time on earth. To move forward, we must keep asking and being asked awkward questions. With that in mind, during the rest of the book, I will guide us through nine elements of our faith by providing a 'pivotal' question, the signs of a Christian-centric religion, and the steps we can take toward a Kingdom-centric one.

Secondly, it's an ongoing *possibility*.

You might be struggling right now with basic elements of your faith, and

becoming Kingdom-centric may seem too far a goal to reach. But it is not, I promise you. When Jesus calls us to seek His Kingdom first, He knows we can do it, and He knows it takes time. In fact, in this journey to reframe your Christianity, you may find the solution to some of your struggles.

Therefore, it might be a good idea to ask: *How Kingdom-centric am I?* And for this purpose, I have created a short self-appraisal. This simple tool is not definitive but will be good enough to get you started. You will find the link in the guide at the end of this chapter. You can also retake the test at the end of the book to see how you have changed.

Thirdly, it contains an ongoing *promise*.

Jesus said that *if* we seek the Kingdom of God first, He will give us all we need, which infers that if we do not, He may not. A condition is clearly stated and a promise is made that may not apply to those who are Christian-centric. This may be hard to swallow. Still, Jesus, again speaking to believers, urged us to listen to His words, rather than put words into His mouth, when He said:

> *"If you remain in me and my words remain in you, ask whatever you wish, and it will be done for you."*[13]

'If.'

God loves you, but Christ implores us to listen to how the Kingdom really works! I had given my life to God, not *after* I had been healed, but *before*. It was not the healing that brought me to God but the coming to God that brought me healing! And, as you will see, He brought me to Himself for more than just my personal benefit. In fact, when we dig just a little, we realize that Kingdom-centric Christianity is not simply believing in Jesus but also in what Jesus believes in. It is not only trusting in Jesus but also in what Jesus trusts in. Nor is it wanting only Jesus but also what He wants.

Which, of course, begs the question: *What on earth does Jesus want?* . . .

Recap

Our religion pivots on what we pursue.

- CC: *We pursue our vision, God's way, so He gives us what we want.*
- KC: *We pursue God's Kingdom, God's way, so we give Him what He wants.*

Christian-centricity and Kingdom-centricity are both Christianity. Consequently, we do not seek to be Kingdom-centric to win more of God's love but to better direct our love for Him.

We start by asking: Which of the two religions am I following?

Reflect

Consider the following:

- Do I ever feel that I sometimes miss the point?
- Are my questions like those of a pagan or a pilgrim?
- Is my religion what Jesus witnessed or what He wants?

Respond

Download the guide at kingdom-centric.com to:

- Analyze how Kingdom-centric you are.
- Begin an awkward conversation with God.
- Consider your motives for each of the ten topics.

Explore additional resources:

- Book: *Kingdom Principles: Developing Godly Character*
- Video: Pais Movement YouTube channel, *Kingdom-Centric Series*

02 | Gospel

Balisea

T'shuva

At 5 years old, my eldest son taught me what on earth it is that Jesus wants.

God wants all mankind to repent.

> "This is good, and pleases God our Savior, who wants all people to be saved and to come to a knowledge of the truth."[14]

However, the kind of repentance He desires may not be what we think it is. Its purpose and benefits are far more profound and inspiring than we may have imagined. Understanding this is essential, because the gospel message we believe will shape the repentance we exhibit, the Christianity we follow, and the results we will see.

To explain, let me share what I learned from my then five-year-old son.

One day, I returned home from work to find pink Sharpie scribbles all over my computer screen and its casing. Instinctively, I knew the culprit was Joel; however, to be certain, I decided to use my 'dad' voice. If he cried, I would know he was guilty. So, with a calm but booming tone, I called out:

"*Joeeel!* Come up to my office, please."

Two seconds of silence passed, and then the whimpering started, followed by the crying, and then wailing. As he climbed the stairs, his Auntie Helen, Auntie Lisa, and Auntie Julie, who had been spoiling him rotten in the living room, called to me upstairs, asking me what I might do. I could tell he had them in the palm of his hands. He was working his crowd, using his large blue eyes to plead . . .

"Please don't whip me, Daddy! Don't whip me again!"

By the time he got to the door of my study, he was in that complete state of shock that all misbehaving children go through when they know their end is nigh. Shaking from head to toe, he struggled to get his words out and kept repeating, "I'm sss . . . sorry, I'm sss . . . sorry!" At the same time, I was becoming more and more irate. I told him that he had been naughty, that it was not just my computer, it was the church's computer . . . *it was God's computer!* I admonished him, explaining that the pink marks would never come off, and to demonstrate this fact, I grabbed a piece of cloth and wiped it across the screen.

The pink markings immediately disappeared!

That took me by surprise. What happened next, however, stunned me. In the blink of an eye, Joel changed from a blubbering mess to total elation. He threw his hands up, beamed like a Cheshire cat, and shouted, "Yippee!" as he turned and skipped joyfully out of my office! "Come back here, sunshine!" I called to him: "You still did it, you know!" His reply was simple: "Yes, Dad, but you wiped it all away!" It was the best sermon on redemption I had ever experienced.

But the key is *why* he was rejoicing . . .

Joel was not excited because he would not get 'whipped.' We rarely used physical punishment. His sadness, and therefore joy, came from a different place. My ever-active child had been stopped from playing downstairs with his brother while being overly indulged by my wife's three sisters. And now, he realized he could return to *how things should be*.

Similarly, what can stop us from experiencing the most joy in our connection to God is our limited understanding of redemption. This is largely due to the English word 'repent,' which simply denotes a turning away in remorse. However, the Jewish concept of repentance better explains God's *intended purpose* and is best understood in the Hebrew translation:

    T'shuva: 'To turn and return.'[15]

T'shuva, also written as *teshuva* or *teshubah* and pronounced *tesh-oo-baw*, is derived from the root word used in the prayer of repentance in Lamentations:

    "Turn us to you, O Adonai, and we will be returned."[16]

When researched, we discover that *t'shuva* has a much deeper meaning than simply turning us to God; it implies that we should also return to who God intended us to be and, specifically, to what God intended us to do. However, our modern understanding of the Gospel seems to be missing this second part.

We turn, but do we *return*?

Or do we simply look back on what Christ has done for us, thanking Him for emptying Himself for our sake, but rarely filling ourselves with a vision of what He wants us to do?

Turning without returning has its problems. Do you remember the parable Jesus shared about being set free from the consequences of sin without that next step?

> *"When a defiling evil spirit is expelled from someone, it drifts through the desert looking for an oasis, some unsuspecting soul it can bedevil. When it doesn't find anyone, it says, 'I'll go back to my old haunt.' On return, it finds the person spotlessly clean, but vacant. It then runs out and rounds up seven other spirits more evil than itself and they all move in, whooping it up. That person ends up far worse off than if he'd never gotten cleaned up in the first place. That's what this generation is like: You may think you have cleaned out the junk from your lives and gotten ready for God, but you weren't hospitable to my kingdom message, and now all the devils are moving back in."* [17]

This illustrates an extreme case of turning but not *returning*.

God loves you dearly. The fundamental reason you exist is that God did not have someone *exactly* like you, and He wanted someone *exactly* like you. But He has a greater plan for your repentance than simply rescuing you from the consequences of your sin. Your personality and talents are unique, and He wants you to return all of them to Him; in *that process*, repentance will return you to the 'you' that He had in mind when He first imagined you.

So, what's His greater purpose for that more fantastic plan?

Interestingly, a Jewish teacher of Judaism, with whom I discussed *t'shuva* some time ago, signs their emails with the encouragement:

"Your next action will change the world ~ make it count!"[18]

True repentance, the kind Jesus had in mind, will prompt us to return to who we can be and work to return our world to how things should be.

This is the true meaning of the word *shalom*.

Shalom

Shalom is the Hebrew word for peace and is connected to *shaleim*, which means *completion*.[19] Although used for 'hello' and 'goodbye,' it implies a blessing much more significant and more profound than a simple greeting. As one scholar puts it:

> "We call it peace, but it means far more than mere peace of mind or a cease-fire between enemies. In the Bible, *shalom* means universal flourishing . . . Shalom, in other words, is the way things ought to be."[20]

God wants to make you complete, but He also wants to enlist you in completing His plan for our world. This *intended purpose* of repentance separates the two Christianities. Paradoxically, while the Christian-centric Gospel prioritizes personal transformation, the Kingdom-centric Gospel has a greater potency to do just that because it aligns our lives with His bigger plan!

Therefore, our response to the Gospel pivots on its message:

>Christian-centric: *Jesus came to rescue you.*

>Kingdom-centric: *Jesus came to recruit you.*

This brings me to my second awkward question:

>Which of the two Gospels have you embraced?

Has the Good News only benefitted you, or has it compelled you to bring that same benefit to those around you? Whilst the Christian-centric Gospel prioritizes personal transformation, the Kingdom-centric Gospel requires us to transform our world. God calls us to return to who He created us to be and lead others to do the same, and in this way, we give Him what He wants! To raise our *kavanah*, (a concept we will soon explore), we seek to feel what God feels for the lost in order to share His Gospel with the same passion He has for the world.

If you want to seek first His Kingdom, let me outline how your *t'shuva* can bring about His *shalom* . . . Visit Kingdom-centric.com to see a visual image I created to illustrate this process, and be encouraged that you can make a difference!

1. In the beginning, God created the heavens and the earth. There was purity on the planet, and humanity was sinless.

2. Then, the devil was permitted to influence the world.[21] He is described as 'the ruler of the kingdom of the air'; the New Testament Greek word used here is *archōn* (pronounced *ar'-khone*).[22] We see his impact all around us; it is awful, distressing, and an attempt to destroy many lives, including those you love.

3. Yet, when we repent, submit to the Lordship of Christ, and receive the Kingdom of Heaven, part of the devil's territory and influence is taken away. Remember that the Kingdom of God is *infinite*, whereas the devil's territory is *finite*. When God takes us out of darkness into the light, the devil loses something; it is ripped from him and cannot be replaced.

4. As we work out our salvation and our thoughts and actions align with His, more of the devil's territory disappears as the Kingdom grows within us.

5. What happens next really starts to put the boot in. Just as apples produce more apples and rabbits produce more rabbits, Christians produce more Christians. As we follow Jesus by sharing His Gospel and leading others to Him, the influence of light over darkness multiplies, and our testimony acts as a catalyst to advance His Kingdom.

6. As we disciple those new believers, the Kingdom grows within them, further expanding the Kingdom as they employ God's gifts.

7. When they make new disciples, more of the devil's territory is removed, the Kingdom advances, and eventually, the world will be returned to what it should be!

This is Jesus' intended purpose, in the words of one of His disciples:

> "*The reason the Son of God appeared was to destroy the devil's work.*"[23]

As more and more people come under the Lordship of Christ, joining in His

mission, the picture changes and the devil will get what's coming to him:

> *"Now is the time for judgment on this world; now the prince of this world will be driven out."*[24]

In other words:

8. *Shalom!*

One day, every knee will bow and every tongue will confess that Jesus Christ is Lord, and although my visual illustration may be simplistic, it helps us see how *shalom* will be restored if we seek the Kingdom of God first.

But what exactly is the Kingdom of God?

It was Jesus' favorite topic, and He refers to it over 100 times in the four Gospels. Most Christians I ask can define the 'Church': "It is not a building. It is the people of God." Surprisingly, however, those invited to explain the 'Kingdom of God' often struggle: "Is it where you go when you die?" "Is it the Church?" "Is it heaven?" Some even look confused by the question.

Do you know what it is?

Depending on which Gospel you read, you will find that Jesus referred to either the Kingdom of God or the Kingdom of Heaven; they are the same thing, translated slightly differently. The New Testament Greek word used for Kingdom is:

> *Basileia:* 'Royalty, reiqn, rule, and realm'

Jesus described the Kingdom as being near,[25] here,[26] and still yet to come,[27] which seems a little odd . . . How can it be here and yet near? How can it be now and still to come?

The Kingdom of God is not limited to a time and place; it is *wherever, whoever,* and *whenever* people accept His Lordship. This is better understood with the help of another English translation of Matthew 6:33:

> *"And He will give you all you need from day to day if you live for Him and make the Kingdom of God your primary concern."*[28]

To understand the concept of seeking first the Kingdom, picture a familiar

place—perhaps your local community, school, supermarket, factory, or office. Then, imagine everything in that place is aligned with how things are in heaven, and all the people have come under the Lordship of Christ. What visual images come to mind when you think of Jesus' command to love one another fulfilled in your place of work? What footage do you see when you visualize His grace and mercy dominating your neighborhood? What scenarios play out in your imagination when His level of honesty, integrity, and godliness are duplicated in your local supermarket or place of recreation?

In the Sermon on the Mount, Jesus said that *if* you make this your *primary concern*, you will receive the promise that goes with it. If you do not, of course, you will not.

So, how does the Gospel we embrace help or hinder us in this purpose?

Rescued

Question: *When is the Gospel not the Gospel?*

Answer: *When it's only half the Gospel.*

Recently, while teaching the Kingdom-centric concepts, I was asked an interesting question. A delegate wanted to know if the Kingdom-centric teaching should be reserved for mature Christians and presented only after people had responded to a simpler, perhaps more amenable, Christian-centric Gospel. It was a great question, one that I had never thought of addressing.

So, before I unpack one of Jesus' parables, let me share one of mine:

> To what can I compare the Kingdom of God? It is like a man who dreams of planting an orchard because he needs the nutrients that only apples provide. So he purchases the best seed from the most renowned nursery. A professional horticulturist is then hired to tell him the most suitable place in his garden to plant it. He feeds that seed with the finest fertilizers and faithfully commits himself to the perfect watering schedule. After sprouting, it grows to become a strong tree, and at the right time, it produces a harvest. When it does, the man is excited to reap what he has sown, and as he reaches into its branches, he pulls out . . . the entirely wrong kind of fruit!

Why?

Because you cannot produce apples from an orange seed.

Just as the man tried to grow apples by mistakenly planting an orange pip, a Christian-centric Gospel will not produce Kingdom-centric disciples!

The message of the Kingdom is not the fine print at the bottom of the Good News, and although the 'bait and switch' methodology might work within some business models, it has no place in the Kingdom of God! From the beginning, Jesus made it clear to His disciples what they were getting themselves into, and He discipled them in the principles and practices of the Kingdom. When He sent them out, it was to declare the Kingdom-centric Gospel from the beginning.

> *"When you enter a town and are welcomed, eat what is offered to you. Heal the sick who are there and tell them, 'The kingdom of God has come near to you.'"* [29]

If you have been raised in the Christian-centric religion, can I encourage you to start your spiritual transformation by embracing the Kingdom-centric Gospel? It has always been available to you through the Word of God. However, whether it has germinated, grown, and begun producing fruit depends, not only on the seed, but on whether or not you have been open to hearing it. As an itinerant preacher, I see this very clearly. I can preach the same message in various places but witness multiple levels of response. This is because what is spoken is only as transformative as the receptiveness of the hearer.

Jesus explains this through the parable of the sower.[30]

His story was a rendition of a popular allegory commonly used to describe four types of hearers. Other versions were employed by teachers such as Gamaliel[31] and Philo of Alexandria.[32] Rather than their metaphors of fish and kitchen utensils, Jesus emphasized the type of heart His listeners had by using a path, rocky ground, thorns, and good soil.

He explained its meaning to His disciples in the following way:

First: *The Path*.

> *"Listen then to what the parable of the sower means: When anyone hears*

> the message about the kingdom and does not understand it, the evil one comes and snatches away what was sown in their heart. This is the seed sown along the path."

The first type of hearer does not *perceive* the Kingdom. Without understanding, and therefore retaining mere head knowledge, their hand-me-down faith is vulnerable to the devil's schemes.

Second: *The Rocky Ground.*

> "The seed falling on rocky ground refers to someone who hears the word and at once receives it with joy. But since they have no root, they last only a short time. When trouble or persecution comes because of the word, they quickly fall away."

The second type of hearer does not *pursue* the Kingdom. Uninterested beyond its benefit to them, when challenges arise, they feel its purpose is not worth their pain and so they give it up.

Third: *The Thorns.*

> "The seed falling among the thorns refers to someone who hears the word, but the worries of this life and the deceitfulness of wealth choke the word, making it unfruitful."

The third type of hearer does not *prioritize* the Kingdom. Failing to give it the time and space required to pursue its disciplines, its purpose is suffocated by everything life brings.

Fourth: *The Good Soil.*

> "But the seed falling on good soil refers to someone who hears the word and understands it. This is the one who produces a crop, yielding a hundred, sixty or thirty times what was sown."

Finally, this fourth type of hearer *promotes* the Kingdom. They become disciples who produce other disciples, and in doing so, they increasingly give God what He wants.

The story of the four hearers is the perfect example of why Jesus used parables. *The NIV Study Bible* explains: "Parables compel listeners to discover the

truth while at the same time concealing it from those too lazy or stubborn to seek it." The fact that you are reading this book suggests you are compelled to cultivate its message in your life and the lives of others. I find that incredibly encouraging because I have dedicated my life to converting non-believers to Christ, and now, in order to multiply what I can give God, my desire is also to convert believers to a Kingdom-centric life.

As we are all transformed, we become transformative!

Recruited

Question: *When is the Gospel good news?*

Answer: *When it brings out the good in people.*

Some time ago, I was invited to be a guest speaker at a boarding school in Europe. The school had been established as a Christian ministry, which held weekly chapel services, but no student had made a decision to follow Jesus. I asked permission to share a Kingdom-centric Gospel rather than a Christian-centric one, and graciously, the staff permitted me to do so.

Using Scripture, testimony, and stories, I unpacked the following:

> "Have you ever asked, 'Why do I exist?' The answer is quite simple. You exist because no one exactly like you ever existed before, and God wanted someone exactly like you. You are loved because you were created to be loved. Of course, not everything about you is lovable, is it? We're all flawed and imperfect. In reality, we often need saving from ourselves. Yet, when Jesus came to die on the cross, He did not simply rescue you; He came to recruit you. He came to invite you to spread His love. God says that the kind of religion that He desires is the kind that looks after orphans and widows in their distress and rejects the evil in the world that pollutes us. If you are prepared to do that, to ask for forgiveness, turn from your sin, and follow Jesus, then He will fill you with His love so that you can bring that love to others. Do you have a sense of that already? A bigger reason to live than just you? If so, can I ask you to return to the person He created you to be and live to advance His Kingdom?"

When I invited the young people to respond, two-thirds stood to say yes to Jesus, including every young man! Afterward, a cafeteria lady approached

me and declared:

"If I had not seen it with my own eyes, I would never have believed it!"

The teens in that room responded because a Christian-centric message had seemed disingenuous. It appeared to be religious camouflage for the selfishness they saw in the message they had previously heard: "Follow God and He will give you what you want." However, when the dots were connected between their desire for a sense of purpose and the call of Jesus to destroy the works of the devil, that more authentic message hit home.

So, please stop preaching a Christian-centric Gospel!

It's too finite. Too uninspiring. And, as we will explore further in a later chapter, it may provide the seeds for an eventual loss of faith. Beyond that, it will not bring about the impact you hope to see in your life and those around you. Instead, make the switch and embrace Jesus' Kingdom-centric Gospel. In doing so, you will experience a spiritual transformation that will never come through politics, insurrection, or social reform but through the reframing of your faith!

To illustrate, let me share the story of two communities:

Community One: *Kenyon Lane*.

When we married, my wife and I decided to move into the most deprived area in England.[33] It was where the church we served was located, and although a family friend offered a nicer home at a lower price in a more aspirational neighborhood, we chose to buy a house in the church's neighborhood with the hope of making a difference.

It was a place of great need.

During the eighteen years we served there, two teenagers were murdered. One was intentionally mowed down by a car a few yards from our home, and the other, a sixteen-year-old girl, was burned alive after being tortured for a week in a house around the corner from us.[34] In reaction to this and many other problems, the local government injected millions of euros into our block of four streets as part of a regeneration plan. They gave grants to residents, built a local park, increased security, and improved housing.

According to the city's most prominent newspaper, simply being aware of these issues was going to help the government fix the problem the only way they knew how:

> "[Officials] say that identifying poorer areas in this way will improve their knowledge of where to provide money." [35]

In the book *Kingdom Pioneering: Fulfill God's Calling*, I explain how the government completely rebuilt the home we owned . . . *for free!* And yet, six years later, they bulldozed the entire area because things became far worse than they were before. They had removed the problem but neglected to inject the real solution, and just as Jesus predicted . . .

> " . . . *the devils had moved back in."* [36]

Money, politics, charity, and anything else but the Kingdom is just a band-aid.

Community Two: *Dean Street.*

Around the time the government failed to fix our neighborhood, we were invited to repurpose a church in a community two miles away. We asked the local police where the greatest need was and were pointed to a cluster of streets opposite the church where gangs were harassing residents. The locals had hoped that if they stayed indoors the criminals would pass on by. Instead, the gang members knocked on their doors, and while the families hid upstairs, their harassers would spend the evening watching their television, playing computer games, and raiding their kitchen for food. The people were terrified.

Partnering with our missions organization, the Pais Movement, and another non-profit, The Message Trust, we recruited people who felt so passionate about the Kingdom that they moved into the area to live among the residents. Some rented, some bought homes, and all lived out the Kingdom-centric Gospel. Within a couple of years, the area was completely changed. People came to Jesus, young people were given purpose, and the project even won an award from the Centre of Social Justice for community transformation.

The Kingdom moved in, and the devils moved out!

Although few will be called to move location, a Kingdom-centric Gospel calls us to not only love God but also those He loves . . . those He created.

So, what might it inspire *you* to do?

Responding to this Gospel can be challenging and require sacrifice, so wouldn't it be wonderful if there were a unique catalyst, a kind of fairy dust that can be sprinkled so that we might be more effective and encouraged to pursue whatever the Kingdom-centric Gospel calls us to do?

Well, there is!

But what is it, and how do we attract it?

Recap

Our response to the Gospel pivots on its message.

- Christian-centric: *Jesus came to rescue you.*
- Kingdom-centric: *Jesus came to recruit you.*

While the Christian-centric Gospel prioritizes personal transformation, the Kingdom-centric Gospel requires us to transform our world. God calls us to return to who He created us to be and lead others to do the same. In this way, we give Him what He wants. To raise our *kavanah*, we seek to feel what God feels for the lost in order to share His Gospel with the same passion He has for the world.

We start by asking, which of the two Gospels have I embraced?

Reflect

Consider the following:

- Which of the four types of hearer am I?
- When, if ever, have I shared a bait-and-switch gospel?
- What has the gospel I have shared produced in others?

Respond

Download the guide at kingdom-centric.com to:

- Pursue Jesus' Kingdom-centric Gospel.
- Prioritize Jesus' Kingdom-centric Gospel.
- Promote Jesus' Kingdom-centric Gospel.

Explore additional resources:

- Book: *Shalom: How to Reach Anyone, Anywhere*
- Video: Pais Movement YouTube channel, *Kingdom-Centric Series*

03 | **Righteousness**

Kavanah

Naughty

I backslid in a nightclub at the age of 18.

In Christian terminology, 'backslide' means going backward, regressing, or relapsing. I did less of the Christian disciplines that helped me become more like Jesus: praying, studying the Bible, going to church, etc., and instead of returning to who God created me to be, I became the kind of person I did not want to be. I still identified as a Christian and believed in God. My faith had not changed, but I had stopped pursuing the second part of His command:

> "Seek first the Kingdom of God *and his righteousness* . . .."[37]

The fundamental reason I had ceased to pursue righteousness was that I had not been pursuing it for the right reason in the first place. I had hoped to be righteous for a different reason than God's *intended purpose*. I pursued it much like the pagans had pursued their forms of 'righteousness': to earn the blessings of my God.

I thought righteousness would give me what I wanted.

As a backslider, I disconnected myself from anything that would stir my faith and connected to whatever would sear my conscience. I left the church and purposely spent time in environments that allowed me to do the things I should not do. I became one of the early members of 'The Haçienda,'[38] an infamous nightclub in Manchester, and over time, I decided that I had found much better things to make me happy than righteousness.

It would be three years until I came back to my senses.

The transition in my thinking during those three years roughly mirrored a transformation that had started in the theology of the Jews over four centuries.

To explain their similarities, let me first ask: Is your Bible naughty? There is a page in many printed Bibles that is hugely misleading. You may find it between the Old and New Testaments. If you have a 'naughty Bible,' you will discover the guilty party . . .

A blank page.

That blank page represents approximately 400 years of history. It is deceptive because it gives the impression that nothing interesting happened. No one won a miraculous victory, betrayed anyone, or slept with someone they should not have slept with. It infers that little of significance took place.

Yet nothing could be further from the truth!

During that intertestamental period, something groundbreaking occurred that opened the minds of the Jews to the teaching of Jesus. It became known as 'The New Sensitivity within Israel.'[39] Without it, the followers of God might never attract the 'fairy dust' that would make their service to God effective, but with it, even someone like me could make a difference!

In that era, awkward questions were being asked. The old compensatory law the Jews had adhered to was coming under attack. In the Old Testament, they believed that black was black and white was white. Do something bad, and bad things will happen to you. Do something good, and good things will always be the result. Pursue sin and be punished; pursue righteousness and be rewarded.

This law had a profound effect on their understanding of righteousness!

For instance, in the Biblical story of Job, the devil challenged God, suggesting that Job's faithfulness was not authentic but merely a response to God's blessing on his life. God permitted Job's faith to be tested to prove Satan wrong, which led to great suffering for His servant. This was made even worse when, due to their belief in the old compensatory law, Job's friends wrongly assumed that his adversity indicated hidden sin and so pressured him to confess.[40] They were, of course, badly mistaken.

However, during the New Sensitivity of Israel, grey areas were acknowledged, and the old compensatory law came under scrutiny in the form of three big questions, the first of which was:

> "Is it true that good people always prosper and evil people always suffer?"

Even the psalmists and the prophets had pointed out that this was not always the case,[41] which eventually led the Jews to enquire further:

> "If a man performs a righteous act to receive a righteous reward, is it really righteousness in the first place?"

In the mix was the broader issue:

> "How will our righteousness usher in the Kingdom of God and our salvation?"

None of the religious parties during this time could provide satisfactory answers. Few could explain how what they believed synced with what they were experiencing. It would take God Himself, in human form, to clarify the three big questions being asked at the time of His birth:

> Is the compensatory law correct?
>
> Is righteousness what we think it is?
>
> Is the Kingdom of God what we expect?

All three questions pivoted on righteousness, a concept that God also needed to help me understand because, as it turned out, being righteous was not what I had thought it was. I thought that righteousness was simply moral purity. In my mind, to be righteous was to be holy and pure in my thoughts, words, and deeds. I've since discovered that moral purity is just the *byproduct* of righteousness!

In Matthew 6:33, the New Testament Greek word used for righteousness means something different from what I had previously understood.

> *Dikaiosynē*: 'The correctness of thinking, feeling, acting, purity of life, rightness'[42]

Only part of this description concerns purity; mostly, it's about alignment.

> Righteousness is to be *righted* with God.

It is when we align our will with His will!

But what does that mean, and how does it happen? Well, another benefit of the New Sensitivity era was the permission to ask increasingly awkward questions. The most challenging is so thought-provoking that the rabbis still discuss it today . . .

"Do *mitzvot* require *kavanah* or don't *mitzvot* require *kavanah*?"[43]

Almost everything Jesus ever taught was an answer to that question![44]

Let me explain . . .

Mitzvot

When a Jewish boy becomes a 'son of the commandment,' he has his bar-mitzvah. *Mitzvah* is the Jewish word for a commandment, and the ceremony denotes that the boy is now personally responsible for his relationship with God. *Mitzvot* is the plural of *mitzvah*, so the question being asked is:

"To truly obey the commandments, must we have '*kavanah*' when we fulfill them?"

Which, of course, begs the question . . .

What is *kavanah*?

The nearest English word to describe *kavanah* is 'intent,' but that is an insufficient interpretation of a Hebraic concept that is far more specific and layered.

Kavanah is to '*direct the heart.*'[45]

Although we separate thinking and feeling using the brain and heart to represent these two elements, the ancient Jews did not. When the Bible references our hearts, it speaks of the core of our innermost being, including our intellect *and* emotions.

To possess *kavanah*, therefore, we must have:

An awareness of the *presence* of God in what we do.

An awareness of the *purpose* of God for why we do it.

For instance, the most significant words in this passage . . .

> *"And he took bread, gave thanks and broke it, and gave it to them, saying, 'This is my body given for you; do this in remembrance of me.' In the same way, after the supper he took the cup, saying, 'This cup is the new covenant in my blood, which is poured out for you.'"* [46]

. . . is the proviso: *"In remembrance of me."*

As *kavanah* is to think and feel what God thinks and feels about what we do, and therefore should lead us to do things for the objective He wants to achieve, so then, the ritual of breaking bread is pointless without reflecting on God's presence and purpose. As one rabbi points out:

> "No *kavanah* is demonstrating with my thought that my deeds do not matter." [47]

Righteousness is not that we obey God for His purpose *instead* of ours, but that His purpose has *become* ours! Before I backslid, I fulfilled many of His commands *without kavanah*. I sought to know the do's and don'ts with little thought of how obeying them could fulfill *God's* objectives. However, when I returned to follow Jesus, it became clear that if Jesus were asked, "Do *mitzvot* require *kavanah*, or don't *mitzvot* require *kavanah*?" His answer would be a resounding . . .

> "Yes, they do!"

Jesus was a powerful proponent of *raising kavanah*, and it is the key to almost every parable, teaching, and comment He ever made. It also unlocks the gift we need in order to advance God's Kingdom successfully.

I discovered the reason for this within the repentant petition of King David, a man described by God as having *"a heart after my own."* [48] He also backslid. Then, after committing adultery with Bathsheba, he planned the death of her husband! When God sent a prophet to confront him,[49] David's conviction led to a prayer steeped in *kavanah*:

> *"Create in me a pure heart, O God, and renew a steadfast spirit within me. Do not cast me from your presence or take your Holy Spirit from me. Restore to me the joy of your salvation and grant me a willing spirit, to sustain me . . . ."* [50]

David first directs his heart toward God by asking for greater awareness of God's presence, and as his prayer continues, it demonstrates his awareness of God's purpose:

> " . . . Then I will teach transgressors your ways, so that sinners will return to you."

He knew that God's presence would lead him to God's purpose!

Specifically, he understood that to lead people to God, he would be more effective with the supernatural empowerment that comes from being 'righted' with God, or as one Jewish source describes it, the *"exceptional ability"* that flows from His Spirit.

He knew he needed to be *anointed!*

Anointing is the 'fairy dust' that God wants to sprinkle on all we do for Him and is given when we obey Him for His purposes. The New Testament Greek words for "anoint" means 'to smear or rub with oil,' by implication, to empower for religious service. It signifies the Father's call on a person and the empowerment He gives to those He believes in, those who serve Him in spirit and truth. David knew that with God's anointing, he would be assured that the Father would add a supernatural unction to His thoughts, words, and deeds!

Essentially, *alignment* leads to *anointing*: [51]

> "This is the confidence we have in approaching God: that if we ask anything according to his will, he hears us."[52]

For instance, when we are righted with God in our hearts, thinking and feeling what He thinks and feels, we will more naturally pray for the things He wants and, in doing so, experience the results He experienced.

> "The prayer of a righteous person is powerful and effective."[53]

Anointing may not make what we do for God *easier*, but it will make what we do more *effective!* So to raise our *kavanah*, we focus on God's purpose for any command He gives, believing that we will attract the anointing required to complete it more successfully.

It is important to note that God anoints us not for our sake but for His, and so during my backslidden state, I went through my own 'new sensitivity within Paul' when the Holy Spirit highlighted a conflict between my reason to chase holiness and God's greater purpose for it. This has led me to the following realization.

Our righteousness pivots on our motive for obedience.

> Christian-centric: *We seek His blessing.*
>
> Kingdom-centric: *We seek His anointing.*

And so here is my third awkward question for you:

> For whose sake are you being righteous?

Is your obedience primarily motivated by the desire to be blessed or become a blessing? Are you seeking God to receive a greater abundance of God's gifts or to destroy the devil's work more powerfully? Are you pursuing righteousness for God's sake, to be righted with Him and align your will with His, or are you obeying God purely for your own reward?

It's a tough question, and awkward, because God is not saying one is right and one is wrong, which would be easier to define; He's indicating that one should be our primary intention and the other our secondary incentive. Our personal blessing should be an added bonus to the joy we feel when we get to give God what He wants.

So, how do we discover what is motivating our obedience to God?

Blessing

Question: *When is righteousness not right?*

Answer: *When it is wrong.*

But how can righteousness be wrong?

Desiring God's blessing is not only perfectly acceptable, it is recommended! Jesus encouraged His listeners to seek it and promised multiple blessings when He shared the Beatitudes. However, after promising those blessings,

He reminded them of what should be their primary concern, because He witnessed a pursuit of righteousness that was the antithesis of *kavanah* . . . the misuse of *korban*.

He highlights the problem on another occasion:

> *"You have a fine way of setting aside the commands of God to observe your own traditions! For Moses said, 'Honor your father and mother,' and, 'Anyone who curses their father or mother is to be put to death.' But you say that if anyone declares that what might have been used to help their father or mother is korban, then you no longer let them do anything for their father or mother. Thus you nullify the word of God by your tradition that you have handed down . . ."* [54]

Korban is something good; it denotes consecrating something to God, such as a sacrifice or food offering. Its most precise description is:

> *Korban:* 'to devote to God.' [55]

However, as with all good deeds, *korban* is only credited as righteous when given for the right reason. In Jesus' example, the Pharisees ignored God's command when it did not suit their purpose and instead used a religious act to give God what they should have given to their parents. Among other reasons,[56] this gave them the appearance of generosity and increased their religious status, but it was the wrong kind of kindness.

Jesus did not say *korban* is sinful but used it as a metaphor, adding . . .

> *". . . And you do many things like that."*

Just as *kavanah* is an awareness of God's presence and purpose in what we do, the abuse of *korban* hides our selfishness, using spirituality as the excuse to do whatever we want.

Have you ever done anything like that?

God wants to bless you more than you can imagine, but one of the paradoxes within Christianity is that the less we do something solely for our blessing, the more we are blessed. So, let's examine ways we might miss the point and be misaligned when fulfilling His commandments

First: We may struggle to *feel* what God *feels*.

I recently discussed recognizing God's voice with a German Pais apprentice keen to follow God's direction but struggling to feel His presence. Shortly after our conversation, I was taken aback when he enthusiastically asked me if I had watched certain British TV shows he liked. I told him I had not, as I knew they contained considerable violence, sex, and profanity. I then asked if he saw the connection between his struggle to hear God's voice and opening his mind to material not aligned with God's values. He told me that he did not.

The rabbis asked similar questions:

> "Why do some feel the divine presence and some do not?"[57]

But they admitted the answer:

> "The limitation is with the receiver since the windows of his heart are polluted . . . the more one cleans them, the more light will enter."

The Bible does not tell me what I can watch, what I can listen to, or even where I can go. This freedom purposely invites me to wrestle with God for answers, but it can be misused.

> "'I have the right to do anything,' you say—but not everything is beneficial. 'I have the right to do anything'—but not everything is constructive."[58]

On my return to God, I needed a way to measure what would point me in the right direction and avoid searing my conscience. Fortunately, John Wesley offered a great truth:

> "Worldliness is anything that cools my affection towards God."

So, let me provide you with two helpful questions I now ask when wrestling with what I should watch, hear, and absorb: "Is this beneficial to what God is doing in me?" and "Is it constructive to what God wants to do through me?"

Second: We may struggle to *know* what God *wants*.

That's important. Without *kavanah*, we can make up our own version of righteousness. For instance, many Pharisees believed that God would only send the Messiah once Israel had cleaned up its act.[59] Their pursuit of a 'sinless'

Israel intensified their judgment of sinners and led them to create rules God never intended.

Quoting Isaiah, Jesus said about them:

> "'These people honor me with their lips, but their hearts are far from me. They worship me in vain; their teachings are merely human rules.'"[60]

Again, it is a matter of the heart. Along with the teachers of the law, the Pharisees asserted *control*, whereas Jesus encouraged *culture*. Control uses external influences to repress what is inside us, but culture changes what is inside to influence what is external.

> "Woe to you, teachers of the law and Pharisees, you hypocrites! You clean the outside of the cup and dish, but inside they are full of greed and self-indulgence. Blind Pharisee! First clean the inside of the cup and dish, and then the outside also will be clean."[61]

So, if you want to clean up your words, don't bite your lip; instead, align your heart. In doing so, the words flowing out of you will naturally sync with God's will. Not only that but whatever flows from your lips will then reinforce the change in your heart.

Third: We may struggle to *do* what God *does*.

This may lead to self-righteousness.

> "But seek first his kingdom and his righteousness."

His righteousness. Not your own.

Of all the religious parties of His day, it is argued that Jesus was most closely aligned in purpose with the Pharisees, who also hungered for God's Kingdom. Jesus positively highlighted their teaching, saying:

> "The teachers of the law and the Pharisees sit in Moses' seat. So you must be careful to do everything they tell you . . ."[62]

However, He also said:

> " . . . But do not do what they do, for they do not practice what they preach. They tie up heavy, cumbersome loads and put them on other

people's shoulders, but they themselves are not willing to lift a finger to move them."[63]

We see so much of that exhibited in modern-day life, right? When people 'cancel' others but do little to alleviate the problem themselves. The increase in polarization is uncovering the self-righteousness of mankind, and a new type of secular Pharisee is rising up. One that judges others but does little to collaborate on the problem. It tempts me to question whether their primary intention is to bring change or to feel better about themselves, and I wonder if I sometimes do the same.

Jesus showed us a different path.

We can discover how Kingdom-centric or Christian-centric we are by asking, Do I mirror Jesus' righteousness or mimic the Pharisee's self-righteousness?

>Righteousness: *"This is wrong, so I will make it right."*

>Self-righteousness: *"This is wrong, so you should make it right."*

The good news is that God works with us, even when we get things wrong. Look at those He chose to do His work! David, Gideon, Paul, and Peter struggled with sin but were moving towards God's purpose. This provides a hugely important insight into the nature of the Father and who He chooses to anoint:

God does *flawed*; what He doesn't do . . . is *fake!*

Anointing

Question: *What is the one thing Jesus never healed?*

Answer: *Character.*

Jesus healed the sick and the oppressed in an instant, but spiritual transformation takes time, and the Apostle Paul reminds us that once God does His part, we need to do ours:

>*". . . continue to work out your salvation with fear and trembling, for it is God who works in you to will and to act in order to fulfill his good purpose."*[64]

So, let me give one ancient practice the rabbis still use to train their disciples.

'Questions of *kavanah*' are awkward questions we ask ourselves and are a traditional method by which we can determine how to become more 'righted' with God. Let me present a couple of classic Jewish examples and two of my own.

First: *The Matzah question.*

Quoting from Jewish tradition, I heard a rabbi present his disciples with the following question: "A Jew went to the bakery to buy his favorite bread, but when he arrived, all the bread was gone except some unleavened loaves. As there was nothing else, he purchased one. When he returned home and started to eat, it suddenly occurred to him that it was the day Jews were only supposed to eat unleavened bread. Did he fulfill the commandment?"

What do you think?

The rabbi and his disciples agreed he did not.

Second: *The Milk question.*

The rabbi then asked a slightly more complex question: "An Orthodox Jewish father was holding his baby as a pot of meat was cooking on the stove. To check the temperature of the milk in the baby's bottle, he splashed a few drops on his wrist. This action accidentally caused a few drops of milk to spill into the cooking pot. Did he violate the commandment prohibiting Jews from cooking meat and milk together?"

The students and rabbi agreed that he did not because milk can be cooked with meat without infringing upon Kosher laws if it is in tiny quantities.

Immediately, the rabbi presented a follow-up scenario to his students. In this case, the father, enjoying the added flavor, deliberately allowed four or five drops of milk to fall into the simmering meat. Once again, the question was raised: "Did he violate the commandment?"

This time, the rabbi and his students answered with a resounding 'yes!' Why? The amount of milk had not changed, but the direction of the man's heart had.

Third: *The Integrity question.*

Here's one of mine: "A man attracted to his female colleague decided he would attempt to seduce her and, in preparation, booked a hotel room. However, when he arrived at his place of work, he discovered that she had been transferred to another office, and he had missed his opportunity. Did he commit adultery, yes or no?"

If you said yes, you agree with Jesus, who taught: *"You have heard that it was said, 'You shall not commit adultery.' But I tell you that anyone who looks at a woman lustfully has already committed adultery with her in his heart."*[65]

Fourth: *The Charity Question.*

Let me ask another: "A Christian lady is walking down the street when she reaches into her bag and accidentally drops her purse to the ground. Without realizing her mistake, she carries on walking. A few minutes later, a homeless man finds the purse and takes her money to buy himself a meal. Did she fulfill the commandment to feed the poor?"

No. There was no intention. It was not a sacrifice; it was an accident.

These questions of *kavanah* can help us align ourselves with God by putting ourselves in His place. I encourage you to create ones that relate to your own life. In this way, you are making yourself aware of His presence and purpose for what you do.

But don't overthink it!

Please don't worry that you will accidentally fall away from righteousness. God has given us His Holy Spirit to guide and keep us on the right track. When I backslid, I did it intentionally. Instead, raise your *kavanah* by committing to the disciplines all Christians should, such as prayer, Bible study, and church attendance. But learn how to pursue them from a Kingdom-centric perspective. In the following three chapters, I will unpack those disciplines, and starting with the Word of God, I would like to ask:

When you read your Bible, what exactly are you searching for?

Recap

Our righteousness pivots on our motive for obedience.

- Christian-centric: *We seek God's blessing.*
- Kingdom-centric: *We seek God's anointing.*

To be Kingdom-centric is to pursue righteousness for God's sake rather than our own. It is to be righted with God, and as we align our will with His, we attract God's anointing to serve Him more effectively.

We start by asking, for whose sake am I being righteous?

Reflect

Consider the following:

- Do I struggle to feel what God feels? If so, why?
- Do I struggle to know what God wants? If so, why?
- Do I struggle to do what God does? If so, why?

Respond:

Download the guide at kingdom-centric.com to:

- Become more aware of God's presence.
- Become more aligned with God's purpose.
- Become more aligned with God's practices.

Explore additional resources:

- Book: *Kingdom Principles: Developing Godly Character*
- Video: Pais Movement YouTube channel, *Kingdom-Centric Series*

04 | **Bible**

Haverim

Intervention

I returned to Jesus on a double-decker bus when I was 21.

In the three years I backslid, I had sought independence. I left home so my parents could not tell me what to do, I left the church so my pastor could not tell me what to do, and I stopped praying so God could not tell me what to do. Eventually, I moved into a two-story house containing four apartments. I shared one on the lower floor with another backslidden Christian. Opposite us were three wealthy students; above them lived a Jehovah's Witness plus a rather dramatic hippie, and above me lived three anarchists and a ferret.

It was an interesting time.

We often discussed our diverse worldviews. The students were hedonists, the anarchists were militant vegetarians, and everyone had strong opinions on life's purpose. Sadly, my lifestyle seriously undermined my ability to sway them toward the Christian message, and they did little to convince me of their beliefs. I was becoming set in my ways, so my return to Jesus began like any other Wednesday. I was sitting on the top deck of a double-decker bus on my way home from my parent's house, where I had taken my dirty clothes to be washed by my mother (I never really figured out the independent bit). While looking aimlessly out of the window, something happened to me that would change my life forever . . . a kind of spiritual intervention.

Suddenly, I felt God's presence fill my entire body as though it was being poured out of heaven, and an incredible sense of joy washed over me.

Then, five words dropped into my head:

"*Paul, do you remember this?*"

"Yes," I thought . . . "Yes, I do!"

I not only remembered God's presence, I realized just how much I had missed the overwhelming sense of peace it can bring. Immediately, I asked myself: *"What am I doing?!? Why am I still running away from God's will?"* The presence of the Holy Spirit was so powerful that it beat any argument I could possibly put up, so there and then, I decided to recommit my life back to Him. Actually, for some strange reason, I decided to wait until the following Sunday to go to church and 'make it official.'

This time, however, I wanted a new kind of relationship.

In my pre-backslidden Christianity, I could not say I was truly in love with God; I was just following Him out of duty, but now, I wanted to do it right. So I had to ask myself:

How do you fall in love with someone?

The answer, of course, is spending time with them. Even when falling in love is not your intention, spending time in someone's company can create a strong connection. This is especially true if you have a common bond, such as a job or project. How often do we hear stories of adultery, such as a boss having an affair with their colleague or a vicar running off with their secretary?

Presence founded on *purpose* is a heady mix!

The decision to recommit my life to God therefore required me to resume my spiritual disciplines, those I had dropped like pieces of litter on my journey away from God. But this time, I would engage with them from a different perspective, one more Kingdom-centric, that would draw me deeper into His presence and purpose. The first of these was to study God's Word regularly, and in my Bible, there is a passage of Scripture with a particularly interesting heading: 'Warning Against Falling Away.'

It reads:

> *"In fact, though by this time you ought to be teachers, you need someone to teach you the elementary truths of God's word all over again. You need milk, not solid food! Anyone who lives on milk, being still an infant, is not acquainted with the teaching about righteousness."* [66]

There's that word again.

Remember, to be righteous is to be 'righted,' to be aligned with God's purposes. That is why the writer of Hebrews goes on to say in the next sentence:

> *"But solid food is for the mature, who by constant use have trained themselves to distinguish good from evil."*[67]

Note the key . . . *trained*.

To become 'righted,' we must stop *trying* and start *training*. Reading Scripture to get a 'word in season' won't do the trick. Bible study is a discipline, not a lucky dip. Suddenly plunging into the Bible to ask God what we should do when we need an answer is a poor way of discovering God's will and a wholly ineffective way to build a relationship with Him.

Previously, I had read the Bible to discover the do's and don'ts. Returning to Jesus, I realized I needed to search the Bible for more than just His *instructions*; I wanted to understand His *intentions*. But surprisingly, I found I could not discover His purpose by simply reading His words — it required something more . . .

Do you remember the WWJD bracelets?

The idea was to wear inexpensive jewelry on your wrists as a visual prompt before making daily decisions. The WWJD motif encouraged us to ask ourselves: *'What would Jesus do?'* I loved that concept. Whoever came up with that idea should have been given a medal, but I have an issue with the wording:

> "What would Jesus do?"

My question is this: Which Jesus?

My Jesus or your Jesus? We all have a slightly different version of Jesus in our heads. My Jesus would do what I want Him to, and yours would likely do what you would like Him to do. Therefore, when we read His words, we interpret them accordingly. To fall in love with the *real* Jesus, a more authentic but perhaps less enigmatic question is required . . .

> 'What *did* Jesus do?'

What Jesus *did* helps us understand what Jesus *meant* by what Jesus said.

His actions are less open to interpretation than His words, and spending time studying the context in which He spoke provides us a better foundation to discover what He wants. We must remember that *He* is the Word, and His example is unambiguous.

> "In the beginning was the Word, and the Word was with God, and the Word was God."[68]

If I was going to advance His Kingdom, I needed to understand the King.

Dwelling

I have no royal blood, just an extremely loose connection to a monarch.

On my mother's side, I am a Munro, a Scottish clan whose allegiance to their sovereign was legendary. As told in the story of the Battle of Bannockburn in 1314, Chief Robert Munro led the clan in support of King Robert the Bruce, a well-loved ruler. As he died, the king asked that his heart be cut out, embalmed, and given to a worthy knight who would take it to Jerusalem. His friend Douglas took up the challenge and wore it in a container around his neck. One day, when backed into a corner by their enemy and defeat seemed imminent, Douglas ripped the heart from around his neck and held it up for all his men to see. Then, with a huge cry, he threw it deep behind the enemy's front line and shouted:

> "Fight for the heart of the king!"

Game on.

I can imagine those fanatical, fiercely loyal knights bonded together over time by pledges and oaths, watching in desperation as the heart of their king was thrown into enemy territory. I can envision what must have stirred within them. The passion! The anger! The rage! The spirit! What fighting must have ensued in their quest to rescue and retrieve that symbol of all they believed in and fought for!

The heart of Robert the Bruce is entombed in Melrose Abbey, Scotland.[69] Dead and buried, it will never be fought for again, whereas the heart of the

King of Kings is alive and well.

But who will fight for it?

To know how to fight for what is in God's heart, I knew I had to approach the Bible from a different perspective, and over time, I created a diagram to help me focus my search for God's intentions. I will describe that diagram below, but I encourage you to visit Kingdom-centric.com to download it. Over the years, this simple tool has helped me better direct my heart toward God, and I hope it may help you do the same.

1. Imagine a horizontal line. This line represents God's laws, known as *halakha*, which is the list of commands that teach us 'the way to behave.' God's law is important! We cannot embrace His attributes without obeying His absolutes.

2. Now imagine an 'X' to the left of the line and a checkmark to its right. The 'X' represents the laws we want to avoid breaking so we do not suffer the consequences of sin, and the checkmark represents the laws we must fulfill in order to receive a reward for our obedience. Some people focus on the line when reading the Scriptures to determine what the law tells them they should and should not do. Their search is driven by their fear of getting things wrong and a desire to do the right thing to get the best that God has for them.

I call this 'line-dwelling'.

Using the Bible primarily for finding ways to avoid punishment and earn rewards leads to a Christian-centric religion. In some cases, even legalism. Yes, God's law will help us understand where we are failing, which is extremely helpful, but it does not have the power to help us succeed. It is like a man who takes his valuable but broken car to an auto repair shop where the mechanic plugs it into a computer to run a diagnostic check. The computer may highlight where the problem is, but it cannot fix it because only the mechanic can do that.

So, what's the alternative?

3. Well, imagine a cloud above the line. In the Bible, the cloud is constantly used to represent the *presence* of God.[70] In my illustration, the cloud also

represents *haggadah*, the stories, illustrations, and parables that give insight into the *purpose* behind God's laws and, ultimately, His heart.

I call this 'cloud-dwelling.'

Cloud-dwelling focuses our religion on why God gave us the laws in the first place, and this diagram constantly reminds me to do the same! It drives me to pursue a more Kingdom-centric relationship because to raise our *kavanah*, we need to know God's purpose for the commandments we live by.

Line-Dweller or Cloud-Dweller; which describes you best?

In the Second Temple period, some teachers concentrated on teaching *halakha*, and others on *haggadah*. Jesus was primarily a teacher of *haggadah* and rarely tackled issues of *halakha* without first being asked a question by those listening to Him. I am not for a moment arguing that *halakha* is any less important than *haggadah*; after all, how can you live above the line if there is no line to live above? But Jesus constantly redirected line-dwelling questions by drawing people towards the presence and desires of God that were hidden from them in His Word.

Therefore, our Bible study pivots on where we are looking:

Christian-centric: *We search for what is in God's hands.*

Kingdom-centric: *We search for what is in God's heart.*

And so here is my fourth awkward question for you:

What are you looking for when you study the Bible?

As a six-year-old, I gained an early insight into this pivot from my first girlfriend, Tracey. Our whirlwind romance lasted two full days. It finished when she brought me a miniature parachutist. Do you know the type I mean? A cheap toy made of green molded plastic, a couple of inches tall and wrapped in a transparent cellophane wrapper. When I threw the soldier in the air, the parachute would pop open, and he would glide slowly to the floor. It was brilliant; I mean, who needs an XBox?! I immediately thanked her and quickly ascended the steps of our outdoor garage, where I dropped it from the roof and watched it fall gracefully to the ground.

I was so excited!

Over the next twenty minutes or so, I constantly ran up and down those steps to launch it time and again. Eventually, I turned to look for Tracey, but she had gone! My mother told me Tracey had left because she was upset that I was more interested in her gift than in her.

Lesson learned.

God invites us to study His Word, not simply for the gifts He has for us, of which there are many, but to better understand what we can give Him. The Bible is a treasure trove of old truths to be reminded of and new secrets to be revealed. These secrets will appear to us when we search the Bible to discover what He wants and the greater purpose He has for the teaching we live by. We therefore raise our *kavanah* by studying His Word for the intention behind His instructions and commit ourselves to helping others discover it also.

And this raises an important concern . . .

Hands

Question: *When is Bible study not Bible study?*

Answer: *When the Bible is not studied.*

In some churches, Bible studies have become people studies. Dumbed down and orientated around a video or book, we comment on a passage without the tools to examine it, and everyone shares their opinions. The problem is clear: instead of learning God's thoughts, we study each other's thoughts. In doing so, we also miss out on the process that helps us determine if our interpretations are correct, never mind in line with God's intentions. Just like the readers of Hebrews, could we be accused of spiritual immaturity?

> "We have much to say about this, but it is hard to make it clear to you because you no longer try to understand."[71]

Perhaps without realizing it, Christian leaders have elevated listening to sermons over personal study. This is due to prioritizing church attendance, while Bible study outside of a church program becomes an optional extra.

The result is that some Christians rely solely on the interpretation of their leaders and their relationship with God has become vicarious. We may not live in the Dark Ages anymore, a time when God's people were restricted to only hearing Scripture through ordained priests, but when it comes to exploring the Word of God, we live in the days of willing ignorance.

We live in the 'Dim Ages.'

And do you recall from Hebrews 5:14 who it is who can no longer *". . . distinguish good from evil"*?[72]

It was not those who lacked teaching, but those who did not *train themselves*! So, what are the signs and implications of a Christian-centric view of the Bible, where we receive instructions but do not search for intentions?

First: *We misunderstand what the Bible is.*

Perhaps the greatest example of a Christian-centric religion is how the Bible is pitched to us. It is described as 'a handbook to life,' a spiritual self-help book. Of course, *"All Scripture is God-breathed and is useful for teaching, rebuking, correcting and training in righteousness."*[73] However, if God wanted to write a book of easy instructions, I believe He could have done a better job. When I study the Bible, I leave with more questions than when I began!

Why is that?

At home, I have an instruction manual for the printer I purchased; because I do, I never need to contact the person who made it. I'm not interested in him or why he invented the printer. I just want a simple guide to make my printer work for me. In my Christian-centric mindset, I had a similar desire; I craved a simple answer book to simple questions. In that way, I could 'operate' God.

But the Bible never says it has all the answers!

Written by Jews who typically learned more from Q & Q than Q & A, the Bible reads us as much as we read it. Used correctly, we discover a two-step process, whereby it first poses questions to reveal the areas of our thoughts, words, and deeds that are not yet aligned with the Father. Then, with the Holy Spirit's prompting, we are led to realign those areas with His will. Through this provoking and prompting, we become 'righted' with Him.

Second: *We misjudge what the Bible expects.*

Have you ever fallen for the oldest trick in the book? Excusing our actions by claiming ignorance. Apart from being a citizen of the Kingdom of God, I am also a citizen of the UK and now the USA. When we emigrated in 2005, I had to quickly play catch up because I immediately became responsible for knowing the country's laws. The legal term for this is *"ignorantia juris non excusat,"* a Latin phrase that translates as "ignorance of the law excuses not." This principle is based on the idea that the law applies equally to all individuals, regardless of whether they know its contents.

The same can be said for the principles of the Kingdom of God.

God does not engage with us based on our denomination or religious upbringing. He is not Baptist or Pentecostal. He is not an Armenian or Calvinist. He is not Catholic or Protestant. He will only engage with you based on the principles of His Kingdom, not those you were taught or raised with. We might think that just because Christians around us are doing A, B, or C, it provides a reason for us to blindly do the same . . . but it does not. God will bless, discipline, reward, or remove things from our lives based on His never-changing truths, not the behavioral trends that influence the church. We must, therefore, train ourselves to distinguish between a truth and a trend.

Have you ever done what you were told was right but got the wrong result? If we do not search for His heart, we may be influenced too easily by the hearts of others. So, always remember that the consequences of our actions, positive and negative, are determined by God's principles, not those of your spiritual leaders, the books you read, or the podcasts you hear.

Third: *We miscommunicate what the Bible teaches.*

Imagine a world where everyone did exactly what Jesus told us to do! It would be a nightmare, wouldn't it? Have you read some of the things Jesus said?

> *"So if your eye—even your good eye—causes you to lust, gouge it out and throw it away. It is better for you to lose one part of your body than for your whole body to be thrown into hell."* [74]

> *"And if your hand—even your stronger hand—causes you to sin, cut it off and throw it away. It is better for you to lose one part of your body than for*

your whole body to be thrown into hell." [75]

I have no intention of doing any of that!

Without taking personal responsibility to discover what is in God's heart, we may be led to believe and then pass on false information. By missing God's direction, we may misdirect those He leads us to. And that's a problem, because the Bible is not just *for* you; it should flow *through you*!

Heart

Question: *When is the Bible a great compass?*

Answer: *When it is used as a guide.*

The purpose of the Bible may not be a simple instruction book, but it is certainly a tool for helping others advance His Kingdom. As the father of modern missions, William Carey said:

> "To know God, we need an open Bible and an open map." [76]

Imagine how the Kingdom might grow if every Christian knew how to study the Bible and used Bible study to help their neighbor, family member, or colleague find God. That is God's goal! This is what He wants, and you can direct your heart toward this purpose in three ways.

First: Use it to *tell others*.

At school, when teachers were delayed, we played a game while we waited called 'Crucify the Christian.' It was just a bit of fun unless you were the only Christian in the class, which I was; therefore, I was promptly hung up from the ceiling or buried under tables and chairs . . . by my friends.

However, being the only Christian in my class did have one advantage.

My classmates were skilled at finding and exploiting a teacher's passion. They used these topics to divert them from teaching so the rest of us could chill. One teacher loved Bolton Wanderers Football Club, but another, a biology teacher, had major issues with religion, and my friends distracted him by mentioning my faith. This made me a valuable asset to my classmates, but it backfired one day when all the rooms in 'lower school' were locked, and the

biology teacher had to open them for hundreds of waiting boys. He decided to delegate his responsibility and shouted, *"Oi, Christian. Come and get the keys!"* For the next two years, I heard mocking calls of "Christian" whenever I stepped onto the lower school campus.

Then, one day, something special happened.

In biology class, my faith was yet again brought up, and after a fairly heated discussion, my nemesis said, "Anyway, even if God does exist, as long as I'm a good person, I'll go to heaven." I replied, "No. The Bible teaches Jesus is the only way." This clearly surprised him, and taken aback, he silenced the room with the stunning statement . . .

> "I don't believe you. But if you show me, I'll become a Christian here and now!"

All eyes were on me as I searched for the appropriate verse but could not find it. I tried, but I had yet to be trained. Eventually, nervous laughter broke out as the teacher resumed the lesson, shrugging off whatever God was doing in him. That moment will stay with me forever.

Jesus did say:

> *"I am the way and the truth and the life. No one comes to the Father except through me."* [77]

But how can people believe if no one tells them? And how can we tell them when we are not trained to handle His Word for *His* sake?

Second: Use it to *train yourself.*

One of the huge benefits of studying the Bible for ourselves is hidden within the verse that encourages us to do it.

> *"In fact, though by this time you ought to be teachers, you need someone to teach you the elementary truths of God's word all over again. You need milk, not solid food!"* [78]

The Greek word used in this verse for 'elementary truths' is:

> *Stoicheion:* 'rudimentary principles that march in rank' [79]

The great thing about learning spiritual principles is they teach you how to think, not simply what to think. Looking for straightforward answers to specific questions will only help you in your present situation. However, once you learn a principle, it will help you in multiple situations. Jesus had only three years to teach the disciples, and that is not enough time to have taught them everything they needed to know. So He taught them Kingdom principles, which they could apply to the many issues and decisions they would face.

It takes practice to discover a principle because principles are found within patterns, and noticing patterns requires gathering lots of information, which takes time and intention.

This is why Bible study is a discipline.

Like me, I imagine you don't remember most of your meals, just the special ones. In fact, right now, my wife (the Foxy Lynn, as I call her) is baking a Christmas cake. It's a two-month process and compliments her wonderful Christmas dinner with all the British trimmings. It's one of the many meals I remember, but I eat two or three meals daily and remember very few. Now imagine if I only ate the memorable or exceptional ones; I would likely die of starvation. It's the same with Bible study. If we only read the Bible for its standout verses on special occasions, we will succumb to a slow death from spiritual starvation. Instead, we must consistently absorb the necessary nutrients God puts in front of us to learn and discern.

Third: We use it to *train others*

Over the last 30 years, the organization I have the privilege of leading has recruited thousands of young adults and placed them on the mission field. In that time, I have noticed that the Biblical literacy of those joining us has decreased year after year. Fewer are coming to us from churches that have equipped them with a passion or process to discover the Word of God; instead, the prioritization of church attendance has emphasized a great worship experience.

The result? Many love to sing, but few love to study.

With this in mind, while examining the rabbis of the Second Temple period, I stumbled upon remnants of a methodology closest to how Jesus examined and discussed Scripture. It is a great fit for a generation that wants to pull

information, not have it pushed upon them. I also discovered that this methodology was designed to pass on what was being studied *as it was being studied*. Therefore, because equipping the saints is one of the most effective ways I can give God what He wants, I created an order to the process and named it 'Haverim,' the Hebrew term for friends who study together.

Of course, the Holy Spirit may not lead you to create a Bible study method, but is there one you can adopt and pass on? Feel free to use mine. Haverim is both a book, a free video series, and a downloadable template.[80] Whatever you use, be encouraged; you don't need to be an expert to teach the Word of God; you just need to pass on whatever you have learned. In doing so, you will help train yourself.

After all, to teach is to learn twice!

This mindset of 'giving, not just getting' is also at the core of another spiritual discipline I had to reestablish . . . one which I was reminded of rather rudely!

Recap

Our study pivots on where we are looking.

- Christian-centric: *We search for what is in God's hands.*
- Kingdom-centric: *We search for what is in God's heart.*

God invites us to study His Word not simply to discover the gifts He has for us, of which there are many, but to better understand what we can give Him. Therefore, we raise our *kavanah* by studying His Word for the intention behind His instructions, and we commit ourselves to helping others discover it.

We start by asking: What am I looking for when I study the Bible?

Reflect

Consider the following:

- Have I misunderstood what the Bible is?
- Have I misjudged what the Bible expects?
- Do I miscommunicate what the Bible teaches?

Respond

Download the guide at kingdom-centric.com to:

- Tell others.
- Train myself.
- Train others.

Explore additional resources:

- Book: *Haverim: How to Study Anything with Anyone*
- Video: Pais Movement YouTube channel, *Kingdom-Centric Series*

05 | Church

Ethos

Spur

I refused to preach in church until my mid-twenties.

By then, I estimated that I had shared the Gospel approximately 800 times in schools or on the streets of Manchester. However, I had no desire to do the same within the congregation I belonged to. That is, until my friend asked me an awkward question: Had my pastor invited me to preach in church? I let him know that he had, but that I had decided not to accept his invitation because of my concern that I would not be good enough.

He seemed shocked. *"Wow,"* he replied. *"You're so full of pride!"*

Confused, I explained that I was actually being humble. He begged to disagree, insisting I cared more about what the congregation thought of me than how I could serve my church. He was, of course, totally correct. I used 'humility' as a spiritual camouflage to hide my insecurities. Convicted, the next time I was asked, I said yes.

My initial reluctance to preach reflected the Christian-centric mindset that had made church all about me. God's greater design for the church, a community to serve rather than be served, was not on my radar. It would take time to change my heart, but more than that, it would take a certain type of discipline.

I believe in the local church. For thirty-plus years, I have recruited, trained, equipped, and mobilized young adults to serve in local congregations. Many are now pastors, vicars, youth pastors, and elders, some holding key positions within their denominations. I have led churches, repurposed churches, and planted churches. I believe the local church is one of the greatest inventions of all time.

In fact, I cannot see how I can be Kingdom-centric without attending church.

> *"And let us consider how we may spur one another on towards love and good deeds, not giving up meeting together, as some are in the habit of doing, but encouraging one another . . ."*[81]

Where I have used the word discipline, the Bible uses 'habit.'

> *Ethos:* A habit, custom, or manner for which we do something.[82]

Both go hand-in-hand; it takes discipline to form a habit and a habit to create discipline.

But the word 'habit' has a dual meaning and ironically highlights a problem whereby a church is seen as the place to receive an ongoing and ever-increasing spiritual high. Many churches 'trade' on this premise because, in our consumerist society, church leaders feel pressured to provide the best product they can. In extreme cases, some have become like a business, competing for customers who choose which church best provides their drug of choice. But, as with all highs, you need a stronger shot each time to get the same level of 'hit.' Consequently, it may not take a lot to break that habit if your commitment to the church is based on the need to keep *receiving* something.

The COVID-19 pandemic highlighted this.

The global lockdown broke people's ritual of church attendance, and some never recovered. According to recent studies, since the pandemic, 10% percent of Christians in America no longer attend church in person or online, and 20% of those that do are doing so less frequently.[83] Only 61% of people have stayed in their church, 23% swapped churches, and 16% stopped attending in person altogether. The Barna Group refers to these people as 'Holders,' 'Hoppers,' and 'Drop-outs.'

Lockdowns allowed us to think through our commitment, and the consumeristic message that attracted people to church . . . backfired!

But why?

Here's an early clue. When the Barna Group asked millennials why relatively few were attending online streamed services, the conclusion they came to was pretty simple:

"They don't want to sit back on the couch and fade away; they want to be active."[84]

We are encouraged to attend church for our *personal benefit*: "A church alive is worth the drive." But God's intention for us to be part of a congregation is greater than ourselves. So when the pandemic broke our habit, some found ways to keep their connection to God that suited them better, and others dropped out because it gave them an escape from a commitment or situation they were already struggling with.

Interestingly, I always interpreted the command to *'spur one another on'* as inspiring or encouraging someone. In truth, the original New Testament Greek word, translated in Hebrews as 'spur,' is more combative than I thought:

Paroxysmos: 'to incite, to provoke, to irritate, to cause violence.'[85]

To spur is to challenge one another to do greater things, which can be uncomfortable and lead to conflict. An example of this is when Paul and Barnabus argued. The book of Acts tells us: *"They had such a sharp disagreement (paroxysmos) that they parted company."*[86] Realizing this prompted me to research all the incidents I could find recorded in the New Testament that took place within the four walls of a synagogue or building where the believers were gathered to worship. I found that a clear majority involved friction. Of the twelve incidents I found, eleven mention arguments, disagreements, or violence, and only one depicts a time when believers met and no dispute occurred! I understand that most of the time, things were probably fine; after all, bad news travels faster than good news, but it does pose a question . . .

Why go to church at all?

If there are more effective things to do, more pleasurable places to go, and less frustrating people to be around, then why bother? If our vicars, pastors, and priests tell us that church is for our personal and spiritual growth, why attend regularly when we can stay at home, watch online, or connect with a handful of fellow Christians with a similar outlook?

As a Christian leader, I have to ask myself, have we misspoken?

Audience

At the root of many an untruth is a specious statement.

The word specious refers to something that has the ring of truth about it but, when examined, is found to be false. For example, a teaching that has infiltrated many churches regarding worship is the phrase:

> 'An audience of one.'

Like many a poor idea, this popular concept was created with good intentions. It teaches we should only live our lives for God's approval and not that of others. However, it is often used to encourage believers to focus solely on God during worship and not be distracted by the opinions or expectations of the congregation.

On the surface, most of us might say *'amen.'*

But should we?

When I think about 'an audience of one.' I struggle to find a Biblical basis for it. I am told the phrase is inspired by Jesus' words in Matthew 6:1-8. But scriptures taken out of context and extrapolated to fit other contexts are rarely helpful. Yet, the concept prompts some worship leaders to encourage us to:

> "Block out the people around you and focus on Jesus."

However, the entire point of the church is to do just the opposite!

God intends that we meet to build each other up and build something good together. We can focus on ourselves and have alone time with God at any point during the week, but when attending church, we should invest in each other as we focus on Jesus. In fact, the more I focus on Jesus, the more it leads me to focus on others.

We should not attend church for an audience of one but an audience of everyone!

Sadly, 'an audience of one' defeats God's purpose, and, once again, it comes down to *kavanah*, the direction of our hearts. Indeed, we should not give money, pray, or worship God to impress others. But, we should be very conscious of the positive impact our giving, praying, or worship is meant to

have on the people around us. We must, therefore, ask ourselves *who* we attend church for. This is because *why* we attend church, *how* we attend church, and even *if* we attend church will be influenced by the perspective of the two Christianities.

Essentially, our church attendance pivots on who it benefits:

> Christian-centric: *We go to consume.*
>
> Kingdom-centric: *We go to contribute.*

Which leads me to ask you my fifth awkward question:

> For whose sake are you attending church?

Please don't say 'God.'

God is everywhere. You don't need to pay Him a visit, and He doesn't feel lonely when you don't turn up. You are not doing Him a favor by going to church, nor are you doing yourself a favor if you go for the wrong reason. No, in His eyes, if you are to give God what He wants, you should enter a church to benefit me, and when I enter, it should be to benefit you. Therefore, to raise our *kavanah*, we focus on what God feels about His Church so that we attend with the same passion He has for His people.

At the heart of His perspective lies an important principle, one that can dramatically affect your relationship with God and how He engages with you:

> *Your commitment to Christ is seen by Christ through your commitment to the body of Christ!*

Why?

Because God's commitment to the world is seen by the world through the body of Christ.

> *"By this everyone will know that you are my disciples, if you love one another."* [87]

Since God sees the Church as the bride of Christ, allow me to use my marriage to unpack that principle. I have been married to The Foxy Lynn for 36 years, and we are blessed with two incredible sons and three wonderful

grandchildren. I love my family more than anything in the world! But do they sometimes embarrass me? Of course, they do. Do they sometimes let me down? You bet. So imagine that one day, after speaking at a conference, a delegate comes up to me and tells me how much he loved my talk and how convinced he is that we should be good friends. He offers to take me out to lunch but wants me to know that he thinks my wife is annoying, my kids are brats, and my grandchildren are ugly. Then, he tells me that he would like to spend more time with me but have little to do with them . . . and asks for a hug!

He may get a physical response, but it might not be one he expects.

Of course, this is a ridiculous and hypothetical situation. Or is it? How do you think God feels when we ignore the presence of His children to focus on Him or even leave a church because we fall out with our brother or sister and blame them for our lack of faith?

Consider the following scriptures:

> *"Whoever claims to love God yet hates a brother or sister is a liar. For whoever does not love their brother and sister, whom they have seen, cannot love God, whom they have not seen."*[88]

> *"Then the righteous will answer him, 'Lord, when did we see you hungry and feed you, or thirsty and give you something to drink? When did we see you a stranger and invite you in, or needing clothes and clothe you? When did we see you sick or in prison and go to visit you?' The King will reply, 'Truly I tell you, whatever you did for one of the least of these brothers and sisters of mine, you did for me.'"*[89]

> *"Religion that God our Father accepts as pure and faultless is this: to look after orphans and widows in their distress . . ."*[90]

> *"For if you forgive other people when they sin against you, your heavenly Father will also forgive you. But if you do not forgive others their sins, your Father will not forgive your sins."*[91]

> *". . . for the sake of his body, which is the church."*[92]

When I say that our commitment to Christ is seen by Christ through our commitment to the body of Christ, I am not simply referring to how often you go to church. I'm highlighting that how we engage with His children is taken very

seriously by Him, and if you want to give God what He wants, it's going to take giving those He has created what you have.

Is that principle as close to your heart as it is to your heavenly Father's?

And how would you know?

Consume

Question: *When is attendance not attendance?*

Answer: *When we are not attentive.*

As followers of Jesus, we cannot rely on man-made institutions with their inevitable inefficiencies to keep us focused on the real reason to go to church. A Christian-centric church will not produce Kingdom-centric attendees, and so in the Kingdom-centric church teaching, I address how leaders can change this. Ultimately, however, we are responsible for our own alignment with God and, therefore, we must look for opportunities to serve, not simply be served. To help you decide if the following Christian-centric traits are evident in your own life, I will lead you through three questions:

First: Have I prioritized *benefitting* over *bringing*?

I cannot find a single verse in the Bible that references attending church to receive something, but many highlight the purpose of *bringing* something.

> "When you come together, each of you has a hymn, or a word of instruction, a revelation, a tongue or an interpretation. Everything must be done so that the church may be built up."[93]

Although we are all on a sliding scale between contributing and consuming, if we buy into the idea of an audience of one, we may find ourselves committing to a church based on the quality of what it offers us rather than the opportunity to serve. Or, as in the case of my reluctance to preach, because I believed I would not benefit from the approval of others, I was not prepared to give them what I had.

Second: Have you prioritized *services* over *serving*?

Years ago, my family and I spent four weeks in Barbados, where we experienced a unique type of worship. The format involved well-choreographed

singing items, which could last 10-15 minutes or even longer if the audience participated. The style and lack of a predetermined duration made it unpredictable and exciting!

Upon returning to England, I spoke the following weekend at St. Andrews University Chapel in Scotland, and the contrast couldn't have been greater. Steeped in tradition, St. Salvator's Chapel is where British Royals who study at the university[94] attend church. Constructed in 1450 before the Reformation, it provided a magnificent setting. I was led into the service as part of a procession of professors wearing traditional outfits, hats, and robes, carrying staffs with rich historical significance. The only singing item was performed in Latin, and we worshipped God with ancient hymns.

The contrast of these "opposite weekends" was impossible to miss. And as I pondered which of them I preferred, a question popped into my head: *"Does it really matter?"* If one style caused me to worship God more than another, the thought came to me: Am I worshipping *God*, or am I worshipping *worship*?

True worship is when we serve God by praising Him in front of everyone as a witness to who He is. If your worship of God in one service is more enthusiastic than in another, what does that teach you about your spiritual maturity and relationship with God?

Third: Have you prioritized *religion* over *relationships*?

While attending a training course for those wanting to go into the mission field, I made two friends. Gary, a recent convert to Jesus who had been a male prostitute in London, and Frank, a devout and long-term Christian. I got on well with Gary and Frank, but they did not get on well with each other. They were opposites that did not attract. Gary was rough and ready and did not take himself too seriously, while Frank enjoyed studying the deeper things of God and would spend hours alone praying in a small closet.

Although they struggled to see the good in each other, on the last day of the course, Gary made an authentic attempt to put his relationship right with Frank, wishing him the best for the future and patting him on the back. An hour later, he was in tears, feeling like a failure because Frank had complained to the course leaders that Gary had attacked him spiritually by patting him on the back where "*. . .there is no spiritual armor.*"

I learned a couple of lessons from Gary and Frank.

First, Frank clearly believed in an audience of one. In his mind, he could have a great relationship with God but a poor one with those God loves. Secondly, although Frank continued to lock himself away in prayer, isolating his relationship with God, Gary, who had a rough start, improved in his relationship with those around him. I've since realized that maturity is reflected not so much in where we are in our relationship with God, but in which direction we are going.

Contribute

Question: *When does the church disciple us?*

Answer: *When it is a discipline.*

Practice may not make *perfect*, but it does make *permanent*.

If you want to seek first the Kingdom of God, forming certain habits can be super helpful. They may not turn you into the 'perfect' Christian, but they will turn something that feels unnatural into something that becomes second nature. One such discipline is attending church. It's a habit that can shape our character and connection to God. If we want to become more Kingdom-centric, constantly going to church for a Kingdom-centric purpose will, over time, cement that mindset and renew our minds. So, here are some suggestions.

First: Contribute *unconditionally*.

In God's mind, He gave you gifts in the form of talents and abilities to bring freely without strings attached. They are not bartering chips that you hold back until your Lord or leaders do what you want.

> "Let the message of Christ dwell among you richly as you teach and admonish one another with all wisdom through psalms, hymns, and songs from the Spirit, singing to God with gratitude in your hearts."[95]

Paul, who as a prisoner may have felt well within his rights to sulk and take his ball home, instead emphasized that we are to give everything from the *gratitude in our hearts*. In doing so, he demonstrated that the greater the appreciation we have for what God has done for us, the bigger the gift we will give Him.

And as we know from the 'Seek First' principle, we can never outgive God!

Another parable I like to tell highlights this:

> To what can I compare the Kingdom of God? It is like the king of a country which was in drought and who sent messengers to decree throughout the countryside: "Bring whatever water you can give for those who have none." On the given day, everyone in the Kingdom came to the castle with as much water as they wanted to give. Some brought it in barrels, some in buckets, some in jars, and some in an egg cup. All were asked to pour their contribution into the well where it would later be distributed to those in need. The king was so pleased with the response that he opened the huge doors to his treasure room and said: "Feel free to take home as much as the container you brought can hold!" Some took barrels of treasure, buckets, and jars, but some only had egg cups.

Likewise, when it comes to engaging with His people, God will respond to your level of *kavanah*. The bigger your heart, the smaller your conditions, the greater He will anoint and increase what you bring.

Second: Contribute *inconveniently*.

During the growing awareness of racism in recent years and the various debates around it, Christians have responded in multiple ways, some good, some not so good. Perhaps the most authentic response I saw was from some friends of mine who, after spending some time in thought and prayer, realized that their business employed few Black Americans. This was not by choice but because many of their staff were recruited through the relationships they had built at the church they attended. So, they decided to join an almost entirely Black church. Although it was not their preferred style of church, the hope was to make new relationships that would naturally lead them to offer more Black Americans new career opportunities.

That type of decision may be one that few of us are called to take. But how might we follow their example of putting others before ourselves when attending church?

Let me offer one elementary example . . .

Be on time.

I cannot tell you how often I have brought or seen non-believers come to a service a few minutes before it starts and enter an almost empty room. Do you have any idea how awkward that makes them feel? And what conclusions it might lead them to?

According to a clinically trained chaplain at a renowned psychiatric clinic:

> "Consistent tardiness is the first outward sign of a selfish person."[96]

That makes sense. If the church is all about me, I can turn up whenever I want. If it's more convenient to grab a coffee and walk in late, so be it. However, true compassion is the willingness to allow our personal agenda to be shaped or changed by the needs of others. As we spiritually mature, we become more aware of how our decisions impact others and their journey toward God.

Third: Contribute *intentionally.*

When we direct our hearts rather than have our hearts direct us, we become more proactive in our worship of God, and He loves it!

> *"Speak to one another with psalms, hymns, and spiritual songs. Sing and make music in your hearts to the Lord."*[97]

Notice the phrase: '*Make* music.'

When love is genuine, it is often creative. Think about it: When you receive a greeting card, such as a thankyou note, what are you most interested in reading? The printed words, created by a professional writer and placed neatly within it? Or the message the giver thought up themselves and wrote alongside it? You may be interested in both, but I would suggest that most of us are keen to read the personal note. It may not be as eloquent and even suffer from poor handwriting or grammar, but you know it is written . . . *from the heart.*

Why would God be any different?

It's great that talented people have written beautiful songs to unite us in our worship, but let's not rely on them. Go off-script and give God your thanks in your own words. You may not be as eloquent or elaborate as the skilled worship leader or choir director, but it will mean a lot to your heavenly Father and perhaps spur those around you to do the same.

KingdomCentric

Why not intentionally pray for people at church without being told for whom and when you should pray? How about spending time before a service asking God whom you can encourage? Or find the time after the service to share with someone, giving God the glory for something He did in your life during the week?

Purposefully attending church to contribute rather than to consume has been vital to my ongoing spiritual transformation. Plus, when we discipline ourselves through proactive actions, we rewire our thinking.

However, the discipline that has realigned my thinking the most was not reading the Bible or attending church. It is the one that changes everything and the most obvious place to start our spiritual transformation . . .

Recap

Our church attendance pivots on who it benefits:

- Christian-centric: *We go to consume.*
- Kingdom-centric: *We go to contribute.*

As we become more Kingdom-centric, we can have alone time with God wherever we like, but we attend church to give rather than receive. This involves investing our time, energy, and talents to build something good together with others. To raise our *kavanah*, we focus on what God feels about His church so that we attend with the same passion He has for its purpose.

We start by asking: For whose sake am I attending church?

Reflect

Consider the following:

- Have I prioritized *benefitting* over *bringing*?
- Have I prioritized *services* over *serving*?
- Have I prioritized *religion* over *relationships*?

Respond

Download the guide at kingdom-centric.com to:

- Contribute unconditionally.
- Contribute inconveniently.
- Contribute intentionally.

Explore additional resources:

- Book: *The Shapes Test: Discover Your Shape to Shape Your World*
- Video: Pais Movement YouTube channel, *Kingdom-Centric Series*

06 | Prayer

Amidah

Imagine

I saw my first miracle on a mission trip in my early twenties.

I will share that story later, but whenever I do, it brings back memories of how frustrated I used to feel during the prayer services I attended as a young man. On Tuesday nights, missionaries occasionally visited and shared about their work, often including stories of God's incredible power and provision. Those evenings were inspiring but left me asking: Why do I not see those things happen in *my* life?

The Oxford English Dictionary defines a miracle as:

> "An event that seems impossible and is attributed to a divine agency."

Answered prayer may lead to supernatural healing, heavenly provision, or unexplainable changes in circumstances, but it also serves another purpose. It gives an insight into the Kingdom of Heaven . . .

Miracles are object lessons.

For example, the healing of someone's body demonstrates the restorative nature of God and the making of everything new again.[98] Similarly, divine provision (such as the feeding of the 5,000) points to heaven's abundance and our eternal well-being.[99]

But there is more.

Miracles also affirm who the Father's children are and how well He cares for them. As people witness our prayers being answered, they can see His faithfulness toward those He loves. Of course, God can also be glorified in difficult times, yet the Bible often points to those He has blessed as illustrations

of His goodness.[100] Therefore, as you seek the Kingdom first and God fulfills His promise to bless and provide for us, others are able to observe a heavenly Father lovingly intervening in your life. They may not fully understand it, but they will notice it. I wonder if you have ever had a non-religious friend or family member remark on how obvious it is to them that "someone is looking after you!" I have.

In fact, just recently, a family member literally rubbed me for luck! To help their child in a sporting event, they took a piece of his equipment, and before I knew what was happening, they brushed it against me, telling their son that they believed doing so might help him win. As bemused as I was, it reminded me of something a colleague said while praying for me a long time ago: "Paul, I get the impression of a glass bowl being placed over you, as though you are a specimen in a laboratory. I believe that God is saying that if you seek His Kingdom first in all you do, He will make you an example of how much He will bless those who do likewise."

That makes sense to me. Just imagine the glory we could give God if our prayers were seen as successful! So, here is my question: If it is in God's interest that our prayers are not only answered but *seen to be answered*, why is it that sometimes, maybe even often, they are not?

Earlier in my relationship with God, my prayers seemed especially 'hit-and-miss.' I thought the problem was my lack of faith or that I simply had too little of it.

How wrong I was!

> Jesus said: *"I say to you, if you have faith like a grain of mustard seed, you will say to this mountain, 'Move from here to there,' and it will move, and nothing will be impossible for you."*[101]

God is keen to answer our prayers, and only a modicum of faith may do the trick. Realizing this has helped me understand the reason for my ineffective prayer life. I had been looking in the wrong place, and instead needed to prioritize what God is focused on:

Not the *amount* of faith but the *assimilation* of faith.

To be righted with God, our prayers must be aligned with His objectives and in

sync with His desires. Then, rather than stressing over how much we believe, we can begin to experience the following promise:

> "The prayer of a righteous person is powerful and effective."[102]

But what does assimilation in our prayer life look like?

Faith

To answer that, let me hand over to Jesus who was asked what at first seems a rather strange request:

> ". . .one of his disciples said to him, 'Lord, teach us to pray . . .'"[103]

Did the disciple honestly not know how?

Of course, he did! Jesus' closest followers grew up in the Orthodox Triangle on the north shore of Galilee. As a practicing Jew, the disciple would have been more familiar with prayer than many modern Christians. So, why did he need to ask? Well, note the rest of the disciple's request:

> ". . . just as John taught his disciples."[104]

It turns out that *"Rabbi, teach us how to pray"* was a standard request during the Second Temple period, and Jesus was expected to do something other rabbis did for their followers. But what? Well, again, studying the context helps. The Jews had, and still have, certain regular prayers, including the *Amidah*,[105] a long and rather articulate set of eighteen benedictions that can take some time to recite. A common practice was for disciples to ask their rabbi for his condensed version to understand what was most significant. Americans might call them, 'The Cliff Notes of the *Amidah*.' These paraphrases highlighted what their rabbi believed was most critical to God.

So, the question Jesus was being asked was this:

> "Can you teach us what you consider most important in our prayer?"

When He replied, notice the first petition Jesus put on His list:

> "Your kingdom come, your will be done, on earth as it is in heaven."[106]

According to Jewish scholars, a careful examination reveals that *'your*

Kingdom come' is an exhortation meaning, 'Rule, God, over more and more individuals!'[107]

In what we call 'The Lord's Prayer,' Jesus emphasized that the kinds of people who will make up the Kingdom of God are those who pray for His Kingdom to come, even before their daily bread. This starkly contrasts with my early Christian-centric prayer life, where I prioritized personal needs and rarely prayed for what was most on God's heart:

> *"Ask the Lord of the harvest, therefore, to send out workers into his harvest field."*[108]

I eventually realized that my prayer life should first focus on what God wants: people who do not yet know Him to come to know Him. This should be the first thing on my mind and the first thing on my lips.

Is that how you pray?

When you gave your life to Jesus, did you realize it included giving Him your prayer life?

Just as consistently attending church for God's purpose will realign your overall will to His, so can praying regularly for His desires rather than our own. It's a wonderful thing to know He has given us this incredible opportunity to partner with Him and impact the world rather than leaving things to 'chance.' In fact, it is in prayer where we can again see the contrast between a pagan and a pilgrim:

> Pagans live by fate; pilgrims live by faith.

For example, in ancient Roman and Greek pagan beliefs, fatalism was often depicted as the Moirai (Greek) or Parcae (Roman), a trio of sisters controlling human destiny.[109] As pilgrims, however, we are called to live by faith, not by fate. But where does faith come from?

> *"So then faith comes by hearing, and hearing by the word of God."*[110]

Therefore, our prayer pivots on what we have faith for:

> Christian-centric: *For what we hope.*

> Kingdom-centric: *For what we hear.*

And so, here is my sixth awkward question for you:

> Which of the two faiths are your prayers built upon?

Are they driven by what you hope will happen or what you know God wants to do? Are you hoping that if you pray and believe hard enough and long enough, God's plan will align with yours, or do you pray in such a way that your prayer life will eventually align with His plan? To raise our *kavanah*, we listen to His voice so we are guided to pray for what will most powerfully advance God's Kingdom in our lives and in our world.

All of this is important because . . .

> ". . . without faith it is impossible to please God . . ."[111]

The great news is that we don't have to be a spiritual rockstar to demonstrate faith; we just have to take Him at His word! But how do we know if we are taking Him at His word or just putting words in His mouth?

Hope

Question: *When is prayer least effective?*

Answer: *When it leads to a loss of faith.*

One litmus test to help us discover if our prayer life is more Christian-centric than Kingdom-centric is to ask how it affects our belief in God. In my experience, the people most critical or hostile towards Christianity often have some form of Christian background or connection. They feel let down by God (or those representing Him) because things didn't work out how they hoped they would or they did not receive what they expected. This can create a vicious circle whereby God did not do what they expected, so they expected less and less of Him.

They hoped, but they did not hear.

The origin of the word *hope* lies in pagan culture. Its root can be traced back to the Proto-Germanic word *hopōną*, which describes anticipating a desired outcome or dearly wanting something to be true. Its origins are connected to the fatalistic beliefs of the Vikings[112] and the Old Norse word:

Hopp: "to leap" or "to jump" [113]

To hope is to jump to conclusions!

The difference between paganistic hope and the faith of a pilgrim is that the former is based on what *we would like* to be true, while the latter must be rooted in what *we know* to be true. The result of a Christian praying in hope rather than in faith is that this wrong kind of belief can injure the most important part of us:

> "Hope deferred makes the heart sick . . ."[114]

This is a problem, as the Bible warns us:

> "Above all else, guard your heart, for everything you do flows from it."[115]

Of course, many factors can contribute to people relinquishing or renouncing their faith, making it a complex issue. I do not wish to diminish any hurt felt by those who genuinely put their faith in God. However, I'd like to highlight three scenarios where a Christian-centric prayer life may harm our ability to direct our hearts toward God and even cause our hearts to direct us away from Him.

First: A *disingenuous* faith.

There is a kind of faith common to Christian-centricity that depends on God fulfilling a list of conditions He never agreed to. This reminds me of a press release by the *Chicago Tribune* many years ago. It announced that the Israeli National Park Authority planned what would have become the world's most enigmatic tourist attraction. Jutting out from the beach in the Sea of Galilee, a submerged glass walkway would provide tourists with a unique experience.

According to the news report:

> "The bridge would be submerged an inch or two under the water in the Sea of Galilee, now called Lake Kinneret," officials said. "The bridge won't have guardrails so as not to ruin the tourist pictures, but lifeguards will be stationed nearby." [116]

If it had been built, tourists would have appeared to be walking on water, but, in reality, something unseen would be holding them up! Similarly, we may

appear to be walking by faith, but only if certain invisible conditions are met. These requirements, unseen by others, may include the provision of finances, a desired outcome, or popular support. It is possible that we may not even be aware that we have these conditions in place . . . until they are not met.

Have you made 'deals' with God that He never agreed to?

I encourage you to ask the Holy Spirit to highlight any invisible contracts you may have made . . . and then, voluntarily give them up. In that process, your faith will be refined. If you do not, just remember, for the sake of growing true faith, it is God who removes glass walkways!

Second: A *disappointed* faith.

Recently, I reconnected with a young man who had backslid even further than I had. After some time spent addicted to drugs and alcohol, he shared with me what had gone wrong, explaining how he had followed the teaching of his church:

> *"Paul, I did everything I was told I was supposed to do, but things didn't work out as well as I was told they would."*

Everything he was told to do came with a promise that he would be personally blessed by doing it. He had been led to believe in a modernized version of the old compensatory law. It was an illusion, and when God did things differently from what he was led to believe, he 'lost' his faith. Sadly, he is not the only one.

> *"For the time will come when people will not put up with sound doctrine. Instead, to suit their own desires, they will gather around them a great number of teachers to say what their itching ears want to hear. They will turn their ears away from the truth and turn aside to myths."* [117]

This is why we must ensure our prayer life is not independent of our study life!

Remember, you are responsible for your own religion. A hope, based on the kind of teaching you wish to be true, rather than a commitment to study what is true, may lead to prayers based on the word of a leader rather than the Word of God. When God does not answer them, we may struggle to differentiate the leader from the Lord, and in the process of rejecting the leader, we might also reject the Lord.

Third: A *disillusioned* faith.

If you had met Jesus in the first century, would you have liked Him?

Sometimes, I wonder if I would have. Jesus upset many people because He did not do things as they expected Him to. He upset me when I lost too many loved ones far too early. For example, my father's father, a grandparent I especially loved, lived a difficult life. He was an orphan and, after living through the Great Depression plus two world wars, he lost his eldest son in a plane accident. When he was dying of cancer, he wrote a letter telling me of his fear of death and, just days before I had a second chance to lead him to Jesus, he died. I felt terrible. A few years later, my mother, a wonderful and well-respected lady, also passed away due to a misdiagnosis that allowed cancer to take her life.

Believe me, I understand how grief could turn into a grievance.

However, we are accusing the wrong culprit. Why do we blame God for the evil that clearly falls at the feet of the devil? Perhaps our enemy's greatest trick is to convince us that his work is God's work and vice versa. There is a lot of vice in what the devil has to say, but I am learning that spending time in God's Word and searching for what is in His heart protects me from the devil's schemes.

> *"For our fight is not against flesh and blood, but against principalities, against powers, against the rulers of the darkness of this world, and against spiritual forces of evil in the heavenly places."*[118]

God has put the potential for violence in all of us. It's not a mistake; it's just sometimes misdirected. So when my grandfather died, I went on a mission trip and fought a battle, but when my mum died, I started a movement and went to war.

My question is this: Will you join me?

Hear

Question: *When is prayer most effective?*

Answer: *When it leads to greater faith.*

Faith, as we know, comes by hearing. We start with a bit of faith, and if our prayers are aligned with God's will, He will answer, and we will see the results. Then, witnessing His faithfulness, we are inspired to pray with greater faith and for greater things. It becomes a positive cycle, constantly repeating itself, and is described in the Bible as 'confidence.'

> *"This is the confidence we have in approaching God: that if we ask anything according to his will, he hears us. And if we know that he hears us—whatever we ask—we know that we have what we asked of him."*[119]

'Righted' faith leads to more faith and, as we see our Father answering the prayers of our past, we may find it easier to believe Him in the future. As we do, this growing faith pleases Him, and He recognizes it in a very special way . . .

> *"Abram believed the LORD, and he credited it to him as righteousness."*[120]

So, if the key is not the *amount* of our faith but the *assimilation* of our faith, how do we conform our prayers to grow the kind of faith that pleases God? There are many ways, but let me suggest three practical steps.

First: A transformational *request*.

Science is not anti-faith; rather, it affirms what God has previously said. However, it is often late to the party. For instance, over centuries, it was believed that the following instruction was impossible:

> *"Do not conform to the pattern of this world, but be transformed by the renewing of your mind. Then you will be able to test and approve what God's will is—his good, pleasing and perfect will."*[121]

The idea that we could 'renew our minds' was, at one time, unthinkable. Then, scientists finally discovered neuroplasticity, the ability of the brain to form and rewire neural pathways.[122] In doing so, studies confirmed what the Bible had taught for two millennia. Our brains are not as static as previously thought; our way of thinking can be changed!

The secret? Repetition.

> *"Join with others in following my example, brothers, and take note of those who live according to the pattern we gave you."*[123]

The Greek word used here for 'pattern' is fascinating.

Tupos: a die, stamp, scar; shape, something made by repeated blows[124]

If we consistently choose to think a certain way, it will eventually become natural to us. This is why Jesus recommends that our prayers should always prioritize the following request:

"Your Kingdom come, your will be done!" [125]

By regularly deciding to put His purpose first in our devotional life, our prayers will align us with His will. Not only that, but the more this new pathway is used, the more it will rewire our overall thinking and, therefore, our choices. How great is that? Prayer is the place to be transformed by Him, and its most significant benefit is not provision or even direction, but transformation! Prayer changes things, but most of all, prayer changes people!

Second: A trained *ear*.

Prayer is not just about speaking but also listening. Recognizing His voice is a gift that requires practice. Prudence is needed because when we think we hear God, we must not jump to conclusions. After all, there are three options as to what it might be.

It could be *imagination*, *manipulation*, or *revelation*.

Ultimately, to know if what has dropped into our minds is from God, we need the spiritual gift of discernment, which comes from time spent in His Word and in His presence. However, let me suggest three principles I have found helpful in training my ear to listen for the Holy Spirit's direction. Please note that these are not meant as a comprehensive 'fool's guide,' but they are tools that help me decipher what I hear when I am listening for God.

It could be *imagination* . . .

It may not be wrong exactly, but it could distract you from what God really wants to say. I have found it helpful to notice if what I am hearing is ambiguous or can be put to the test. When it has been God, it often contains something that only God would have known or know how to do.

It could be *manipulation* . . .

You might hope so desperately to hear God say something that essentially you 'make Him' say it, for instance, by ignoring anything that does not serve your purpose. To avoid this temptation, I take notice if what I hear confirms or contrasts with what I know for sure He has previously said. Remember, God uses repetition. Even when He speaks in a new format, something familiar about His message will connect to something you already know to be true.

It could be a *revelation* . . .

An indication that you are hearing God is that it will reveal something that advances the Kingdom even more than you were able to accomplish before. It will be in line with the Bible, in line with His character, and may reveal an answer to the question:

> "What can I do that will most advance the Kingdom of God?"

When all else fails, I have learned a simple litmus test: The Holy Spirit will never lead you to break His Word or your word, and if God is speaking to you, you must act upon it, as it is better not to hear God's voice than to hear it and ignore it.

Third: A trusting *sensitivity*.

Finally, let me tell you the lesson I learned from one of the first miracles I saw. In March 1988, I was within 20 feet of a lady who rose from her wheelchair after enduring 25 years of spinal agony. The tabloid press in England extensively covered the healing as it baffled the medical community.[126] Dr. Colin West, a Jewish physician, characterized it as "unbelievable."

But what did it teach me?

I witnessed this miracle with friends who were amazed by what they experienced but are now backslidden. To my knowledge, none would deny what we all saw, but I learned that supernatural, even dramatic intervention by God is not guaranteed to grow our faith.

Jesus knew this when He sighed deeply, saying:

> "Why does this generation ask for a sign? Truly I tell you, no sign will be given to it."[127]

If we need constant signs to keep our faith alive, what does that say about our trust in God? Revelation without a relationship is the mark of pagan religion. Consequently, I've learned that I must be sensitive to the Spirit in my prayers rather than look for signs and miracles. The influence of circumstantial evidence tends to dwindle over time, but the Holy Spirit is a powerful aid to keep me on the right track. Because of Him, it's hard for us as children of God to be misled unless we want to be. Therefore, if you are prepared to follow His Spirit faithfully, He is more likely to trust you with what He wants to say next. You may even start to hear Him more often than you previously did!

So, if signs are not the best way to receive revelation, what is?

Recap

Our prayer pivots on what we have faith for:

- Christian-centric: *For what we hope.*
- Kingdom-centric: *For what we hear.*

We are called to live by faith, not by fate, and through prayer, we partner with God by putting His purposes first. In this way, we also rewire our thinking to become more Kingdom-centric. Therefore, to raise our *kavanah*, we listen to His voice, so we are guided to pray for what will most powerfully advance God's Kingdom in our lives and in our world.

We start by asking: Which of the two faiths are my prayers built upon?

Reflect

Consider the following:

- Has my faith become disingenuous?
- Has my faith become disappointed?
- Has my faith become disillusioned?

Respond

Download the guide at kingdom-centric.com to:

- Assimilate a transformational prayer life.
- Cultivate a trained ear.
- Develop a trusting sensitivity.

Explore additional resources:

- Book: *Kingdom Patterns: Discovering God's Direction*
- Video: Pais Movement YouTube channel, *Kingdom-Centric Series*

07 | Calling

Lekh lekha

Target

I *think* moving to the USA in 2005 was God's Plan B.

Many years ago, as a young leader, I had the honor of spearheading the transformation of a small UK church that had endured numerous challenges. The opportunity arose when my pastor, Harry Letson, and I recognized that the organization I led required a new headquarters. The number of staff and apprentices within Pais had surpassed the capacity of the church that launched it. Therefore, a local congregation that Harry had been assisting offered its large but deteriorating building to meet this need, under the condition that I would assume leadership of the church.

The next five years were a rollercoaster of a ride!

After some initial difficulties (such as the week I changed the church's name but forgot to tell the congregation), we began to impact our community. I told a little of the story back in chapter two, explaining how we partnered with various agencies and saw spiritual and social transformation in the neighborhood. This caught the attention of the local government, who offered to build a facility for us in exchange for our old, leaky, and high-maintenance property. Their deal came with one condition: that we would extend our work in the community.

It was also the catalyst for a bold plan that I had been working on.

Being a 'local lad,' I had good relationships with the leaders and congregations in my part of Manchester, particularly four small but hard-working churches struggling to make the impact they deserved. I admired each church leader, and all four encouraged me and supported our work in the community. They may not have seen themselves as 'visionaries,' but each had a particular skill

or passion that I believed was undervalued and underused. It became clear that we might be stronger together, so discussions ensued regarding a fairly radical idea.

We would merge for the sake of the Kingdom of God.

Our new purpose-built facility would gather all five congregations on a Sunday to inspire and train them. The four other buildings, all within a radius of two miles, would in turn become mission centers, each replicating the transformational work we were conducting. The other pastors and I would throw our particular gifts and passions into the pot, and thereby the combined congregation would benefit from the holistic gifting of a team of leaders rather than one individual. My role would be to lead the overall work, bringing vision and strategy, and together we would create a working model of an experimental version of the local church. It was a thrilling strategy, and although we were only in the planning stage, our ideas began to permeate through to some of our church members, fueling a growing belief that new possibilities lay ahead!

When my team received the blueprints of the new building from the local government, we prepared to implement the vision. As they say, however, 'the devil is in the details.' After it became more apparent to each leader how our plan would change their role and responsibilities, some of them went cold on the idea.

It was a sad day when we decided, amicably, that it would not work.

As everyone refocused on their churches, I received a request from America offering an opportunity to create a working model of the Pais vision for youth communities by moving our global headquarters to Texas. The idea was pitched to me that while doing this, the church would help us expand the vision of Pais globally through their network. After several months of prayer and discussion with the church team we were leading, Lynn and I decided to take that step.

Of course, the idea that God has a 'Plan A' and a 'Plan B' might be up for discussion. But it seems that because one door shut, God opened the other, and I suspect that if 'Plan A' had gone ahead, we would still be in the UK today.

But what does it matter?

How tied into any particular vision is God's purpose for our lives?

With my early understanding of the nature and intention of God's calling, the fact that Plan A fell apart could have left me wondering: "Have I just missed God's purpose for my life?" and "Will I ever achieve the potential I once had?" This is partly because I saw the vision, or calling, as a target, which prompted questions such as:

"Lord, where should I go?"

"Lord, what should I do?"

"Lord, to whom should I go?"

All in all, any answer I received would be ambiguous. Maybe that is because it's difficult to give a good answer to a poor question. And the kind of questions I asked often missed the true intention of any vision that God had in mind. Perhaps you also are seeking clarity on God's purpose for your life, desiring a specific goal or target for which to aim. It might be a building, number, place, or project. The problem is that these targets can sometimes be man-made and cause any divine calling to become . . . Christian-centric.

In contrast, God's calling on my life does not alter whether I am in England or America because I have come to realize . . .

Vision is best seen not as a *target*, but as a *theme*.

Theme

I make missionaries.

That's my theme. And therefore, it makes no difference where I am. It is not restricted to a particular place or time. I can and should make missionaries anywhere and with anyone. It is how I best show my love to God because, with the gift that God has developed in me over time, it is the most effective way I can give Him what He wants.

So, what is your theme?

In the Old Testament, the Holy Spirit fell on a limited amount of people for a limited amount of time. But it was prophesied that, in the future, God would

pour out His Spirit on all His followers, and all would receive visions and dreams.

> "And afterward, I will pour out my Spirit on all people. Your sons and daughters will prophesy, your old men will dream dreams, your young men will see visions. Even on my servants, both men and women, I will pour out my Spirit in those days."[128]

This prophecy was fulfilled on Pentecost and reminds us that, although our belief in God may occasionally falter, He consistently believes in us! In doing so, He intends to give all His children dreams and visions to advance His Kingdom.

That includes you!

But receiving that vision may be more complex than we think. Although we desire tangible direction, God, in His wisdom, is not always keen to give it. For example, when Peter and Andrew were called to become His disciples, look at how Jesus pitched the idea to them:

> "'Come, follow me,' Jesus said, 'and I will send you out to fish for people.'"[129]

That's not very specific. No place, time, or number is mentioned.

God's call on our life may *appear* straightforward; for instance, Jonah was sent to a particular city,[130] and Moses was given a clear project.[131] But were either of these a calling, or were they simply steps of obedience toward a bigger objective? After all, there was wiggle room in how Peter, Jonah, and Moses could fulfill their duties, and with each one, additional details came later as they kept the conversation of awkward questions going.

Why?

To understand, let's unpack the call of the first-ever pilgrim:

> "The LORD had said to Abram, 'Go from your country, your people and your father's household and go to the land I will show you. I will make you into a great nation and I will bless you; I will make your name great, and you will be a blessing.'"[132]

Even as God told Abram to go somewhere, He didn't tell him where to go!

To pursue the calling he was given, Abram would have to leave everything and almost everyone he knew and loved. God gave him encouragement and a hint of who he would become, but initially, that's about all Abram had to go on. For God to want so much from us and yet be so nebulous with His instruction seems unfair. Why is He purposely vague? Does He simply not have time to give us the specific details? Is it because we are not spiritual enough to hear His voice more clearly? Or, is something else going on?

Yes, there is!

A process for Kingdom-centric formation is hidden within the call of Abram. It comes to light when we discover its context and connect two critical moments: when God first called Abram *and* when He later updated the vision.

The Hebrew term used to describe God's calling of Abram is:

> *Lekh lekha:* 'Go. Leave.' [133]

This Hebrew phrase is not as simple as 'Go;' it has a triple definition. It conveys not only *"Go to yourself,"* but also implies *"Go for yourself,"* and, as some Jewish commentators add, *"Go beyond yourself."* [134] But to really understand the primary purpose of God-given vision, note what happened later in Abram's pilgrimage as our hero received an 'upgrade.'

> *"As for me, this is my covenant with you: You will be the father of many nations. No longer will you be called Abram; your name will be Abraham, for I have made you a father of many nations."* [135]

God attached an initial from His divine name 'YHWH' to 'Abram,' making 'Abraham.' That is hugely significant and crucial to understand! The ancient rabbis teach us that by doing so, the Father's dream had now become Abram's. In renaming Abram, God recognized that on the journey, Abraham had begun to think, feel, and believe what God thinks, feels, and believes. Abraham's heart was becoming aligned with God's.

This is also the purpose of any vision that God gives you!

God wants to shape you for His purpose, and therefore any journey He sets before you is not intended to get you to a particular place, but to bind you to your Father—more specifically, to *His* purposes. In this way, *what He wants will become what you want*. And when that happens—World, watch out!

Our calling, therefore, pivots on what we are focused on:

Christian-centric: A vision of *vision*.

Kingdom-centric: A vision of *God*.

With this in mind, here is my seventh awkward question:

Which of the two types of vision are you pursuing?

Are you excited by God or just by the vision He gives you? Has vision become more important to you than the pursuit of righteousness? Have you found yourself making decisions that limit the advancement of the Kingdom of God to ensure your vision's success?

To raise our *kavanah*, we pursue a greater understanding of who God is in order to allow Him to shape who we can become. In this way, His purpose takes precedence over any goals we have set, and we become willing to sacrifice any element of our vision that hinders the greater good that God wants to do.

After all, wouldn't it be tragic if growing our vision limits His?

Vision

Question: *When is a vision no longer divine?*

Answer: *When it blinds you.*

As we will see later, God will not give you what will become God to you, including a specific calling. You can dream one up for yourself, but then you must maintain it with your own energy and ingenuity. It's exhausting and restrictive. However, when our vision of God grows and all we do is motivated by His ambitions and not ours, the possibilities become endless. So, how can we know if we have succumbed to a vision of vision?

First: It limits *commitment*.

A vision of vision is revealed when we are committed to our thing, not the whole thing. Take, for instance, the youth pastor who is devoted to sharing his faith with those in his youth group but never mentions Jesus to his neighbor.

Or the musician who prepares well in advance, practices her instrument, and turns up on time for rehearsals, but is tardy and unexcited when serving elsewhere. It can also be noted if we are committed to the calling . . . until we are no longer a part of it. Although we once convinced others to get involved, now when it is no longer 'our thing,' we give little thought to it or those we were impacting through it.

In all these cases, we have to ask: Was following our calling ever really about giving God what He wanted, or was it always about fulfilling our own dreams?

Second: It limits *connection*.

As a young man, I thought vision was only given to very spiritual people. Consequently, I hoped that the holier I became, the more dramatically God would speak to me. I assumed that the greater the spectacle, the greater the vision. I soon realized the exact opposite was true!

In many Biblical cases, the more theatrical the revelation people received, the further away from righteousness they were. For instance, Saul, later Paul, was traveling to persecute God's people when:

> " . . . *a light from heaven flashed around him. He fell to the ground and heard a voice say to him, 'Saul, Saul, why do you persecute me?'"* [136]

If you think about it, the reason for this makes perfect sense.

Imagine if I looked for a sign from my wife to know which streaming show she would most like to watch. If she scratched her head when she walked into the room, I would know she wanted to watch the house-flipping program, but if she rubbed her knee, it meant she would be interested in watching cricket. That would be crazy! We have been married for over three decades, and I'm sure she would be upset if I did not know her well enough to figure this out without some kind of signal from her.

Why would God be any different?

Yes, God will provide signs, but they are not how He wants us to build a relationship with Him. Instead, the lack of details He gives actually invites us to search for what is in His heart. Whereas a vision of vision will shortcut that process, a vision of God will lead to intimacy and gradually connect us to

Him. Essentially, the first blinds us, but the second binds us. And so, as I have begun to mature, I find I need fewer signs to follow His lead.

Third: It limits *compassion*.

Compassion is to allow your personal agenda to be shaped by the needs or concerns of others, but a vision of vision tends to be hard-hearted and narrow-minded.

For example, the latest statistics show that 94% of all Christians started following Jesus by the age of 18,[137] which is when the vast majority of young people are in schools. Yet, how much do we prioritize school ministry? If seeking God's Kingdom was our primary concern, serving in schools would be vital to our church agenda. But a Christian-centric Christianity demands that leaders pay greater attention to the needs of their congregation, and school ministry is relegated to a side issue.

The excuse? "It's just not *our* calling."

A vision of vision is behind the religious operating system I have come up against time and again in the last 30 years, and it is being fed by the encouragement of self-help books that tickle our ears and tell us to focus on what we love. Whilst recognizing what switches us on may be a good idea when choosing a career or hobby, applying it to God's calling is disingenuous. After all, Jesus, the greatest of all visionaries, pursued a calling that was never limited to what He wanted to do.

> *"My Father, if it is possible, may this cup be taken from me. Yet not as I will, but as you will."*[138]

Paul also reminded the saints:

> *"I have worked much harder, been in prison more frequently, been flogged more severely, and been exposed to death again and again. Five times I received from the Jews the forty lashes minus one. Three times I was beaten with rods, once I was pelted with stones, three times I was shipwrecked, I spent a night and a day in the open sea . . ."*[139]

Unfortunately, a vision of vision looks for a spiritual excuse to camouflage its true identity; we talk about 'not having God's peace,' but what we really mean

is we don't want to be uncomfortable. As worldliness seeps into our version of godliness, we begin to believe that anything that feels bad cannot be from God, and we resent being asked to do what furthers God's Kingdom if it does not fit within *our* vision. Instead, true vision, the divine kind, will always be bigger than you. It will stretch you to see beyond yourself because God has called all of us to something much bigger than any of us!

With that in mind, let's explore that greater calling, knowing we are far more likely to recognize God's vision for our lives when we understand its true purpose.

God

Question: *When does vision become limitless?*

Answer: *When it's no longer a command.*

Just as Abram's calling was thematic, allowing him to become the father of many nations, when your vision is no longer restricted to a time, place, or person, your ability to advance His Kingdom will become boundless! Therefore, the most significant thing you may ever do may be the one thing no one tells you to do!

> "If anyone forces you to go one mile, go with them two miles."[140]

No one told me to pioneer the Pais Movement. My need to reach out to those in schools was driven by a greater awareness of the pain God feels when those He created to be loved are lost to Him. And it is sustained by my love for Him, not my love for what I do for Him. In fact, I have noticed that the greatest lovers of people are those who love God more than they love people!

Therefore, I've realized that I don't need a bigger vision of vision; I need a bigger vision of God, and I need to 'go' for the reasons revealed in the three facets of *lekh lekha*.

First: *"Go to yourself."*

Ironically, if you focus on God, you will stumble across your true self.

There may be far more of God's character within you than you realize, and if you take a journey toward God rather than toward a target, you will discover

the original you that He wants you to return to. This truth was encapsulated by the author A.W. Tozer,[141] who wrote:

> "What comes into our minds when we think about God is the most important thing about us."[142]

This, he argued, is because whoever you believe God to be, you will gradually become to other people. We see this with the Pharisees, who saw God as a judge and judged people, and also with the Zealots who viewed the Messiah as a warrior figure and became freedom fighters. Similarly, I wonder if how I treat people results from who I understand God to be. Either way, the clearer my vision of God, the closer I will become to the person He created me to be, and the more I will reflect His nature and goodness the way He knows I can.

Not only that, but I will also believe in what He says about me. When I first started my journey, I struggled with doubt. I was unsure I could do what God wanted me to do. I was never one of the cool kids and was expelled from my first school at the age of six for biting my classmates. I had various nicknames that highlighted my slight speech impediment, but as my view of God grew, I realized *"God chose the foolish things of the world to shame the wise."*[143] And my clearer view of God gave me a clearer picture of who He called me to be.

It is also important to note that we are not given vision because we are perfect, but to perfect us. This is obvious by looking at the young men Jesus chose to be His disciples:

> *"He brought him to Jesus. Jesus looked at him and said, 'You are Simon the son of John. You shall be called Cephas' (which means Peter)."*[144]

Again, an imperfect man is renamed and discovers more of His true identity.

Second: *"Go beyond yourself."*

If your aim is to know God rather than simply what He wants you to do, you will discover that falling in love with Him will spur you to go much further than you thought you would.

This was the case in the calling of Moses:

> *" . . . the LORD appeared to him in flames of fire from within a bush. Moses saw that though the bush was on fire, it did not burn up."*[145]

The miracle stopped him in his tracks and was followed by an awkward conversation when God gave Moses the following instruction:

> "And now the cry of the Israelites has reached me, and I have seen the oppression the Egyptians are causing them. So now, go. I am sending you to Pharaoh to bring my people the Israelites out of Egypt."[146]

Moses still resisted; the miracle did not change him, and after citing various excuses, he even asked the Lord to send someone else! Yet years later, Moses was so changed by the journey that, when the Israelites eventually rebelled, he made one of the Bible's most incredible and Kingdom-centric requests . . .

> "So Moses went back to the LORD and said, 'Oh, what a great sin these people have committed! They have made themselves gods of gold. But now, please forgive their sin—but if not, then blot me out of the book you have written.'"[147]

Roughly translated: "Either save them from hell or, if you don't, send me there as well!"

Again, like Abram, Moses became so connected to the nature of the Father, so in tune with His heart, that he was prepared to exceed what was expected of him.

Third: *"Go for yourself."*

A vision of God rather than a vision of vision will lead you to a reward far greater than you realize, one that focuses on the rewards of heaven and goes well beyond the hopes of any earthly pursuit the Lord might give you. Living for these things can bring you far greater joy and, as the joy of the Lord is our strength, it also brings perseverance. But sadly, we can sometimes miss the fullness God has for us due to unfinished thoughts, such as the saying:

> "There is a God-shaped hole in all of us that only God can fill!"

This statement teaches that, although worldly pursuits cannot fulfill us, our Father in heaven can. While I grasp the sentiment, it's not entirely true. The reality is:

> "There is a God-shaped hole in all of us that even God cannot fill . . . in this life."

Why? According to God's Word:

"He has planted eternity in the human heart, but even so, people cannot see the whole scope of God's work from the beginning to end."[148]

God has placed some desires within you that will only be realized in the afterlife. Adopting a more Kingdom-centric mindset may make us feel *less* fulfilled in what this life offers, but it aligns us with God's vision for a Kingdom beyond what we can see. The benefit is that, if our calling leads us to feel what He feels, think what He thinks, and want what He wants, we will gradually experience the delight He has when His Kingdom advances and those He loves return to Him.

Imagine feeling joy like God feels joy!

Finally, pursuing a vision of God is much better than chasing a vision of vision, because even a God-given vision can lead to disappointment when it does not go as well as we hope. And sometimes, it can appear to go very wrong indeed . . ..

Recap

Our calling pivots on what we are focused on:

- Christian-centric: *A vision of vision.*
- Kingdom-centric: *A vision of God.*

Vision is more a theme than a target and, therefore, not restricted to a particular place or time. It intends to bind us to the will of Father so that His purpose becomes our purpose, and we become willing to sacrifice any element of our vision that hinders the advancement of His Kingdom. To raise our *kavanah*, we pursue a greater understanding of who God is in order to shape who we become.

We start by asking: Which of the two types of vision shapes me?

Reflect

Consider the following:

- Does my vision limit my commitment?
- Does my vision limit my connection?
- Does my vision limit my compassion?

Respond

Download the guide at kingdom-centric.com to:

- Discover my theme.
- Go the extra mile.
- Prioritize eternal results.

Explore additional resources:

- Book: *Kingdom Pioneering: Fulfill God's Calling*
- Video: Pais Movement YouTube channel, *Kingdom-Centric Series*

08 | Serving

Ergon

Purge

Everything we had been building almost fell apart in 2020.

At the writing of this book, memories of the COVID-19 pandemic are fading. It was a challenging time for a missions organization founded upon serving public schools. After pioneering the work 30 years ago and laboring each year to reach more and more teenagers, it was a shock to see three-quarters of our members return home when governments called people back, halted international travel, and shut school doors. After pouring our hearts into the work for over three decades, it took only days to be torn apart.

During that time, I was in danger of a problem that caused some to give up . . .

> *"Hope deferred makes the heart sick . . ."*[149]

Sadly, some Christian leaders struggled to keep serving when it looked like their dreams would not be fulfilled. They gave up and moved on. I may not have, but my heart was indeed suffering. Nevertheless, what helped me was a message I had received from one of our alumni. It came shortly before I had heard of COVID-19, knew what 'social distancing' meant, or could even imagine a global lockdown. I had never been sent anything like it, and it even included a title . . .

> 'The Purge'

> "Right before a tidal wave, the waters pull back. We will see signs of God's presence pull back. There is a flood coming. There will be casualties. There will be people whose job it is to protect. There will be people who can't handle the aftermath (confusion) and choose to leave with the wave of water. There were heavenly beings who are sent to help the

casualties. As heavenly beings ourselves, we were able to breathe in the water. But anything not of God was taken. The casualties will be the people who have been leading double lives. Anything not of God will be taken. There will be few left to rebuild. But afterward. Everything was white and pure. There are some casualties who stay to teach others. The ones who were protectors will lead when the waters pass. In the confusion, there will be love and care."

When it arrived, it made no sense. Not only was it abstract in its content, but its doom-laden tone was diametrically opposed to the growth spurt we were experiencing. In fact, I had just met with our trustees to report how well things were going. So, when I read the message, I shrugged my shoulders, forgot it, and left it to gather dust. However, when COVID-19 hit, and the ramifications became evident, I not only remembered it, I began to see it play out!

Although a crisis of epic proportions, none of our Global team or National Directors quit during the pandemic, apart from one couple whose visa ran out. However, that was different for those new trainees recently joining us as part of our gap-year apprenticeship program.

What happened to them was very interesting.

During the lockdown, when schools were shut down and 75% of apprentices were forced to return home, our training department quickly created an online mentoring program. It enables trainees to remotely continue their work with those they used to assist in person. Most embraced the opportunity, continuing to serve teens who now needed their encouragement and direction more than ever. However, some opted out entirely. Once they returned home, they forgot about those they said they felt called to serve.

I used the word 'interesting' and not 'shocking' because this second group did not surprise me. For years, we have realized that two types of people join our apprenticeship program. I am sure both love Jesus, but one type becomes more Kingdom-centric than the other. The majority participate because they aim to serve God, with the bonus of traveling overseas. A minority join to travel abroad, with the bonus of serving God. The pandemic purged our organization of those in this second group, who dropped the young people like bricks when their travel experience was taken away!

Although receiving 'The Purge' reassured me that God had a purpose hidden within what was happening, it left me with a burning question: Could it hold the key to why many Christians are still waiting to experience breakthrough?

Breakthrough

What is preventing the Kingdom expansion we might expect to see?

Whether or not you are personally experiencing spiritual growth, the reality is that worldwide a smaller percentage of the population is following Jesus, and the projections for 2050, provided by the Pew Research Center, show this concerning trend gathering speed.[150]

Why?

Many will lay the blame at the feet of the devil, and to some extent, they are correct. It is undoubtedly true that the sin within mankind has caused people to reject the truth.

> *"The god of this age has blinded the minds of unbelievers, so that they cannot see the light of the gospel that displays the glory of Christ, who is the image of God."*[151]

However, there must be more to the story because Jesus promised:

> *". . . I will build my church, and the gates of Hades will not overcome it."*[152]

If hell cannot stop us, can I suggest that one of the biggest challenges to advancing God's Kingdom lies not in the hearts of those opposed to God, but in how those devoted to Him decide to serve?

Let me explain.

A long time ago, an experienced youth leader asked me to assist him in presenting six lessons over six weeks to 200 students. At the time, I was new to ministry and had zero experience. He assured me this was no problem as he only required me to share my testimony. The first lesson went so well that the principal approached my colleague, asking if he would teach twice as many students the following week. He replied that this would be perfectly manageable, saying: "Paul can teach one-half of the group while I teach the other . . .

Can't you, Paul?"

Blind-sided, I nodded.

I was assured I would get a complete set of notes and be trained beforehand. The following week, I received no training and only fifteen minutes of material for the hour-long presentation. I had to create the rest of the plan independently from scratch. The week after, he informed me that he could no longer commit to the rest of the series and asked if I could continue it for him. This would require me to create and present new material for four more weeks. I would be given the lesson titles but absolutely no content. I was untrained, ill-equipped, and terrified! Wouldn't you be?

But what went through my mind was this:

"If I don't tell these students about Jesus, who will?"

And so, inexperienced and anxious, I did my best. However, if I had been raised in today's increasingly Christian-centric culture, would I have asked a different question . . .

"Is this my ministry?"

Without Christ, those young people would be lost for eternity. They would go through the troubles of this world as we all do, but in the end, they would have no place in heaven. Therefore, as a follower of Jesus, I am commanded to share my faith with them "in and out of season." [153] But is that on the mind of most Christians? Or, after being fed a Christian-centric religion, do we have another priority when it comes to serving God, and if so, to what might I compare it?

Perhaps this . . .

> It is like the captain of a small boat that comes across the Titanic. Upon seeing the men, women, and children drowning in the dark and freezing waters, he begins to motor forward to rescue them. Then he stops. "Hang on a minute!" he thinks. "What kind of boat do I have? Is this a fishing boat? Might it be a tugboat? What if it is a pleasure boat?" And while he is pondering what kind of vessel he has, the people drown in a watery grave.
>
> Why? Because he forgot that, first and foremost, his boat was a boat!

You are called to serve, and your ministry gift is just nuance. It is not your mission. I am not called the lead Pais; I am called, as we all are, to advance God's Kingdom. Leading the organization I lead is simply the most effective way I can think of doing it.

Therefore, our service pivots on our priorities:

> Christian-centric: We prioritize our *ministry*.

> Kingdom-centric: We prioritize His *mission*.

Sadly, I have lost count of the times I have seen opportunities to advance God's Kingdom crushed by those who have put their ministry first.

And so, here is my eighth awkward question for you:

> Which of the two types of service take precedence in your life?

When you serve, are you driven by your love of giving God what He wants or by your love for what you get to do for Him? What has become more important to you: what it achieves or what you do? For instance, if you were given an opportunity to advance His mission more effectively than you can by executing your chosen ministry, which opportunity would you put first?

To raise our *kavanah*, we prioritize God's goals so that the abilities He has given us achieve the purpose for which He gave them. Although the concept of *kavanah* is rarely taught in Christian circles, we are subconsciously aware of it when we employ the term, 'servant-hearted.' This phrase seems to point to the fact that we've always known that the key to good service is to align our hearts. But how should we respond to the opportunities we are given?

For instance, when should we say yes, and when should we say no? And how should we react to needs we notice when we cannot fulfill every need we see?

Ministry

Question: *When is serving God not serving God?*

Answer: *When it does not work!*

What is the point of serving God if it does not give Him what He wants? Another popular, specious statement in Christianity is the concept that "we are human beings, not human doings." Some Christians have taken this mantra, emphasized within existentialism, Buddhism, and transcendentalism, [154] and brought it into Christianity because it sounds 'right.' It has become a trend that lets us off the hook. Yes, we are justified through faith alone, but true faith, the kind God seeks, works!

> "For we are God's handiwork, created in Christ Jesus to do good works, which God prepared in advance for us to do." [155]

This Greek word for 'works' is mentioned 176 times in the New Testament!

> *Ergon:* Work. Deed. Doing. Labor. [156]

God recruited you for a labor of love, not to earn His love but to align yourself with Him in loving the world. Consequently, there are countless Bible verses, parables, proverbs, and psalms in which God is seen to be frustrated with those who do not deliver results. [157] For instance, after cursing a fig tree for not bearing figs, Jesus encapsulates this in the following way:

> "Therefore I tell you that the kingdom of God will be taken away from you and given to a people who will produce its fruit." [158]

Author Lois Tverberg highlights that when Jesus taught, He had in mind the rabbinic term *hasidut*, which asks, "What more can I do to please you?"

> "The [ancient[159]] *hasid* is one who goes beyond the letter of the law in his service of God. He does not do only what he is told, but he looks for ways to fulfill God's will. This requires intelligence and planning; one must anticipate just what God wants of him and how he can best use his own talents in service of his Creator." [160]

She confirms: "God has no interest in senseless service." Therefore, before we unpack how to improve our service, let me give three suggestions for why it can sometimes be so ineffective.

First: Our *feelings*.

I once heard of some wealthy families who were kind enough to respond to a local relief agency's request to care for poorer households during Christmas.

Every year, these sponsors would be assigned to different families and drive them to a nearby supermarket to buy the gifts, decorations, and festive groceries the family could not afford. Then, one Christmas, the supermarket agreed to match the money the benefactors gave. So, the agency turned to its donors and said, "Great news! Instead of taking the families to the store, please contribute directly to us. We will then double the money you give and send the items directly to the needy families!"

Unexpectedly, many of the donors stopped giving.

Perhaps without realizing it, the purpose of their giving had been driven by directly experiencing the gratitude on the faces of those they were helping. When that feeling was taken away, they withdrew their service. Have you ever done something similar?

Second: Our *status*.

A long time ago, while advising a church that wanted to reach the young people of its community, I initiated a teaching series called 'My Generation' whereby a volunteer leader and a youth group member would deliver the sermon as a tag team. I had the pleasure of kicking off the series with my youngest son, who was twelve years old. Together, we studied the story of Abraham and Isaac and unpacked its principles. Then, surrounded by an audience of his peers, he stood on a stage in the middle of the room, and together we shared what we had learned.

He was great.

We both discovered so much, plus he displayed a knack for communicating and a certain 'coolness' in his delivery. The message and method made an impact! The youth were inspired and motivated to step up and share their faith. More tag-teaching happened over the following weeks, and the team planned to use the format several times a year.

Then, out of the blue, we were asked to stop.

The leadership told us that the young people needed to be more spiritually mature to preach. Effectively, we were instructed to halt the on-the-job training of the young people to teach them how Jesus trained His young disciples on the job. I suspect this was to protect the status of a 'professional' ministry.

Jesus found similar insecurities within His disciples:

> *"John said to him, 'Teacher, we saw someone casting out demons in your name, and we tried to stop him, because he was not following us.' But Jesus said, 'Do not stop him; for no one who does a mighty work in my name will be able soon afterward to speak evil of me. For the one who is not against us is for us.'"* [161]

If our priorities are focused on protecting our position and the benefits we receive from it, they will conflict with the opportunity to advance His Kingdom more effectively.

Thirdly: Our *gifting*.

I enjoy the stage. I appreciate a well-built, visually impressive setting. The bigger, the better. I like the opportunity of being in front of crowds and creatively sharing my beliefs. Many years ago, I loved playing guitar in an indie rock band that traveled around local venues and shared the Gospel. We released a cassette that received good reviews and even had our own groupie! (Yep, just the one.) Around that time, the Pais Movement started to grow, and it became clear that time did not permit me to both tour and teach. Although I enjoyed the band much more than leading Pais, it was clear that recruiting, training, and managing hundreds of young missionaries, although stressful, permitted me to be far more effective.

This begs the question.

Could God's calling involve two types of actions: the gifting we love to use and the abilities we dislike using but make what we love to do more effective? Is this what makes our service to God different from the rest of the world? Everyone is happy just to do what they like; the challenge is doing what gets results. Is it this second activity that separates those in it for themselves and those in it for the Kingdom?

What if we took Jesus' words about love . . .

> *"If you love those who love you, what reward will you get? Are not even the tax collectors doing that? And if you greet only your own people, what are you doing more than others? Do not even pagans do that?"* [162]

And apply a paraphrased version to serving . . .

> "If you only do the things you love to do, what reward will you get? Are not even the self-help books suggesting that? And if you only serve those you love to serve, what are you doing more than others? Do not even atheists do that?"

Be encouraged: The more we pursue the gifts of God for His objectives, the more likely we are to receive them! But any other motivation for serving God, apart from serving His mission, will at some point be tested by Him and found wanting.

So, how might we better serve Him in Spirit and in truth?

Mission

Question: *When is serving most effective?*

Answer: *When it asks the right questions!*

If God is not a fan of senseless service, the onus is upon us to determine what being more productive might look like. Let me provide three questions that have helped me decide how to serve Him more effectively.

First: The *Kingdom* Question.

I work with many young adults, and they constantly think about "what next?" to the point that it distracts them from their current work. The silver lining, however, is that the more Kingdom-centric they become, the greater their desire to know *His will* for their lives, which is excellent! What is not so great is when they ask God inferior questions:

> *Where* should I serve?

> *When* should I serve?

> *Who* should I serve?

As I previously stated, I'm not sure God is interested in answering those questions. Instead, I encourage those I disciple to ask what I refer to as the Kingdom Question:

SERVING

"What is the most effective thing I can do to advance God's Kingdom?"

It is a question that has yet to let me down.

At first, you may presume it's a question that should be directed to God, but it is a question I ask myself. Why? Because God invites us to decide what to give based on our understanding of Him. Of course, as we do this in the context of a prayerful life, we train ourselves to better know His intentions on all occasions. So, rather than desperately hoping to find answers whenever we have a choice to make, it is better to stop trying and start training!

Of course, the answer to the question, *"What is the most effective thing I can do to advance His Kingdom?"*, may not be obvious initially. Still, I have found that if I make a mistake, as long as I regularly give time to listen to God, He has always intervened and corrected my direction. As I've previously mentioned, when we have *kavanah*, it's hard to miss the will of God unless you do it purposely.

Second: The *Gospel* question.

It is an aberration to think God's mission is to fulfill our ministry. Instead, our ministry must fulfill His mission. With this in mind, I also ask:

"What will lead the most people into the Kingdom of God?"

In the mid-1980s, my friend Ian and I, both dedicated youth workers, had the idea of a more effective way to impact our city's youth. Initially, we were going to set up a new kind of schoolwork together, but our paths gradually separated over time. I went on to found Pais, and Ian went into politics. Upon reflection, decades later, and after a very successful career serving in the UK, Ian sent me the following email.

> Dear Paul . . .
>
> I looked around at the people that were crammed into the room. I glanced at familiar faces, members of the cabinet, and MPs from around the country. It was 2005, and I was at 10 Downing Street waiting for Prime Minister Tony Blair to arrive. I was there to celebrate a historic third term that the Labour Party had convincingly won. I was proud that I had managed the election campaigns that secured some of the best results in the

country, and I knew that my invitation to Downing Street to celebrate with the party elite only enhanced my growing reputation within it.

The atmosphere was electric; months of round-the-clock campaigning were ending, and it was time to celebrate. Prime Minister Tony Blair and his wife Cherie entered the room, slowly working their way down the line until he stopped at me. *"Hello, Ian; great work with the campaigns. Utterly fantastic,"* he said. Several drinks later and feeling the worst for wear, I returned to my hotel. Lying on the bed, I replayed the last few months and my conversation with Tony in my mind. I am sure you will agree that I should have been delighted and proud of my achievements, but I can tell you I was not. Like most people who get involved in politics, I wanted to help change the world for the good, to make Britain a fairer society for all, and although it was pleasing to see our policy slowly make a difference, I began to really understand that only a genuine spiritual renewal was going to change hearts and minds. Moreover, I began to examine my heart; there was no denying that I had lost my focus, and my walk with God was beginning to suffer. I recalled in my mind and spirit the days, some twenty years earlier, when you and I dreamed, prayed, and dreamed again of what God wanted to do in the lives of the young people of Manchester. Oh, the wonder of it.

The path I chose led me to meet Prime Ministers, Presidents, and thousands of ordinary people, and while wanting to see more Christians involved in the political fabric of our nations, it will never compare to bringing someone into the Kingdom of God. I am now obsessed with the thought that when I die, I don't want my gravestone to say he had so much potential, so much to give. I want that gravestone to say he was a man that served God in his generation. So keep close to God, be honest, and be brave.

Your friend, Ian

People need more than your goodwill; they need His Gospel. So, to serve Him better, ask what is the most effective thing you can do to bring people to Jesus, directly or indirectly?

Third: The *Jesus* Question.

When we choose to serve, we make ourselves vulnerable and we may feel that others are taking advantage of us, especially if we do our bit but others don't do theirs. When this happens, our service to God might be unduly affected by the commitment of those around us. We might ask, "Why should I do XYZ when others do not?" This is a dangerous path to go down because, just as we are accountable before God for our understanding of the Bible, we are also responsible for how we serve Him. We cannot use ineptitude, inaction, or indifference on the part of others to excuse ours. Therefore, I'd like to pass on a principle to combat this:

> The only person you should compare yourself to is Jesus, and the only person you should compete against is yourself!

With this in mind, when choosing how to serve, I encourage you to ask:

> "If I only compare myself to what Jesus did, what should I do?"

Jesus was strategic, intelligent, and committed to serving the Father. Neither feelings, status, nor gifting overrode His decision to fulfill the mission assigned to Him. He learned obedience, even to death on a cross. Now, He asks you and I to serve alongside Him. Some of us have fulfilled some of His mission some of the time, and some have fulfilled most of their ministry most of the time. But imagine what might happen if most of us fulfilled most of His mission most of the time?

We might see the Kingdom come!

I hope you find these three questions helpful in guiding you through the countless opportunities to serve Him best. Most will be so small and incremental that you may never remember nor be appreciated for them.

However, if you're like me, you might recall the decision that shaped all your future ones . . .

Recap

Our service pivots on our priorities:

- Christian-centric: We prioritize our *ministry*.
- Kingdom-centric: We prioritize His *mission*.

God gives us talents and abilities to advance His Kingdom. Therefore, our ministry gift is just nuance, not our mission. To raise our *kavanah*, we prioritize God's goals so that the abilities He has given us achieve the purpose for which He gave them.

We start by asking: Which of the two types of service do I prioritize?

Reflect

Consider the following:

- Do feelings make my service less effective?
- Does status make my service less effective?
- Does my gifting make my service less effective?

Respond

Download the guide at kingdom-centric.com to:

- Answer the Kingdom question.
- Answer the Gospel question.
- Answer the Jesus question.

Explore additional resources:

- Book: *The Shapes Test*
- Video: Pais Movement YouTube channel, *Kingdom-Centric Series*

09 | Giving

Merimnao

Template

In the 1990s, my wife and I made the most significant financial choice of our lives!

After a year of reaching into schools as a voluntary community worker, our church leadership took a step of faith to give me a modest stipend. I was very grateful because I knew how little our congregation had to give, and it showed their commitment to what we had been doing. However, it was not a lot of money, and I remember opening our cupboard one day and realizing we did not have enough food to put a single meal together. I turned to Lynn and asked if she was okay with the situation, saying that if she were not, I would understand and get a secular-paying job.

Her reply has always remained with me:

> "I don't mind how much they give as long as I know it's the best they can do."

Lynn understood the 'Seek First' Kingdom principle: God will always add to whatever is truly given for His purpose. Her selflessness has aided everything we have sought to do and was exhibited in her willingness to live with less income than we might have. Her generosity has also shown itself in sharing me with so many other people. During our thirty-plus years together, she has never once complained about me leaving on a trip to advance the Kingdom or train others to do the same. None of the vision, passion, or strategy we have would have borne fruit if Lynn had not wanted to put the Kingdom of God first in our marriage.

Therefore, in 1992, we made a decision that would become the template for many future ones. As our work expanded and schools opened up, we realized

we needed to recruit more young adults to assist us in reaching our community's young people.

We could fund this in two ways:

First, we could charge a fee to those receiving our training, which would then pay my salary. This was the standard way of framing a Christian internship at the time. However, it would limit the number of those who would be able to join the movement and therefore the young people we could reach.

The second option was to provide our yearly 'apprenticeships' for free, giving participants training, accommodation, and meals without cost. This would increase our ability to gather recruits, especially from less wealthy backgrounds. To do this, Lynn and I would rely on the promise of the 'Seek First' principle for our income.

We chose option two.

Our choice was important because it set a precedent in our marriage, prompting us to make future decisions using the question:

"Where will our giving most advance the Kingdom of God?"

This became our template when determining where to invest our finances, talents, and prayer. So, in 1992, we invested much of ours into founding the Pais Movement. Many years later, we have planted the work in over twenty nations and trained thousands of apprentices and countless followers of Jesus to live life on mission. To some, Pais is seen as a missions organization, to governments, an NGO, while others may label it a para-church ministry. But to Lynn and I, it is simply an overflow of our marriage, an invitation for others to join us as we seek His Kingdom first, and if there is one thing we have learned on our adventure, it is this: You cannot outgive God!

> *"But seek ye first the kingdom of God, and his righteousness; and all these things shall be added unto you."*[163]

We have experienced God's provision in extraordinary, sometimes quite bizarre ways, some of which I share in the book and video series, *The Kingdom Principles: How to Develop Godly Character.*[164] As I have unpacked the first two elements of the Seek First principle, seeking His *Kingdom* and

His *righteousness*, let me now address God's promise to provide "all these things" with what might seem a shocking statement . . .

You don't need to follow Jesus for anything . . . except salvation!

I have met several unhappy believers and many happy non-believers, and both my experience and understanding of Scripture have led me to conclude that being wealthy, healthy, or happy is in no way dependent on being a Christian, never mind seeking first the Kingdom of God.

This is intentional on God's part.

He is uninterested in a purely transactional relationship. Our Heavenly Father wants an authentic one! He desires a friendship whereby what we give Him overflows from our love for Him, not as payment into a divine vending machine.

In saying this, following in Spirit and truth does come with benefits . . .

Worry

Of all the earthly rewards that *seeking first* offers, the greatest is in the mind.

As I've previously mentioned, the one thing God will not give you is the one thing that will become God to you. Of course, you can put aside pursuing His Kingdom while prioritizing finding a spouse, house, career, or success. That's the freedom of will that He has gifted you. But the difference between *getting* something for yourself and God *giving* it to you is simple:

> Whatever you go and get, you must maintain, but whatever God gives, He maintains!

Therefore, down the road of 'seeking first,' you will find peace of mind, something Jesus was keen to highlight when He added the following instruction.

> "... *do not worry about your life, what you will eat or drink; or about your body, what you will wear.*"[165]

At first hearing, this may sound unrealistic. Isn't worrying natural? Well, it does not have to be. Worrying is a by-product of the gift of imagination, and the worst use of imagination is to imagine the worst. Therefore, Jesus' challenge

is actually a piece of very practical advice that is best understood when we examine its root meaning in the New Testament Greek:

Merimnao: 'To divide into segments, to be distracted.' [166]

Jesus was quite literally saying, "Don't go to pieces!"

When deciding what to give, we should avoid dividing our minds in two by negotiating how to simultaneously give God what He wants while equally ensuring we get what we want. This conflict, known as cognitive dissonance, is untenable.[167] It harms our mental health by pulling us in two different directions, and we must decide which to prioritize over the other.

Jesus highlighted this by later saying:

"No one can serve two masters. Either you will hate the one and love the other, or you will be devoted to the one and despise the other. You cannot serve both God and money." [168]

The peace of mind God has for you is based on single-mindedness. As our *t'shuva* brings about God's *shalom* in the world, He offers us robust and flourishing mental health that is based on a different foundation than the one the world has to offer. While Western society promotes happiness, inspired by Hollywood and ratified in the US Declaration of Independence:

"We hold these truths to be self-evident, that all men are created equal, that their Creator endows them with certain unalienable Rights, that among these are Life, Liberty, and the pursuit of Happiness." [169]

God offers something far better:

"Do not grieve, for the joy of the LORD is your strength." [170]

We may presume happiness and joy are similar, but that is a mistake. At least in one way, they are complete opposites.

Happiness is when the *external* influences the *internal*.

It is the result of what happens. When good things happen, we are happy; when bad things happen, we are unhappy. When we are up, we are up, and when we are down, we are down, and those emotions can often impact our

spiritual and mental state. It's bad for decision-making, and, as the Bible teaches, *"A double-minded man is unstable in all his ways."*[171]

Joy is when the *internal* influences the *external*.

It can be experienced when good things happen *and* when bad things happen. It is not based on circumstances but on the confidence that we are in a good place with a good God. This joy, given by His Holy Spirit and craved by King David when he wrote, *"Restore to me the joy of your salvation . . .",*[172] leads to consistent faith and confident decisions.

This is why Paul the Apostle was able to say:

> *". . . I have learned in whatever situation I am to be content."*[173]

Righteousness leads to holiness, and the reward of holiness is wholeness.

As you become more aligned with God and His purposes become more critical, you will give without concern about what you will receive back. In doing this, you will become more confident that He has your back, and you are likely to experience things working out in unexpected ways. This comes when He anoints a generosity that is not tainted by strings we attach to ensure our security nor conditional on God rewarding us.

Consequently, our giving pivots on our motive:

> Christian-centric: *We give to get.*
>
> Kingdom-centric: *We get to give.*

And so, here is my ninth awkward question for you:

> Which of the two motives drives your giving?

Do you give primarily for personal reward or Kingdom return? Is your generosity based on the belief that if you give, you will receive? Or is it a thanks-giving for what you have already been given? Are you giving because you think it will make you happy, or are you giving to what will best accomplish God's purposes?

Whilst giving for personal benefit and God's purposes are both Biblical, the second is more aligned with God's character. So let's unpack both motives in

order to become the kind of givers who give Him what He wants, in the way He wants us to give it!

Get

Question: *When is giving not giving?*

Answer: *When it's not what it appears to be.*

Paradoxically, the more we give without the motive to get, the more we get—which is a little tricky if you think about it! The Bible tells us that it is impossible to please God without faith and faithlessness is at the heart of an entirely Christian-centric form of generosity. To avoid it, let me unpack three signs of 'giving to get.'

First: It is motivated by *image* rather than *impact*.

Remember how Jesus had an issue with the Pharisees using *korban* to disguise their real intentions? We can also thank their hypocrisy for the modern-day phrase 'blow your own trumpet' or 'toot your own horn.'

> "So when you give to the needy, do not announce it with trumpets, as the hypocrites do in the synagogues and on the streets, to be honored by others. Truly I tell you, they have received their reward in full."[174]

Jesus is invoking the image of the thirteen wooden boxes placed at the treasury in the temple, under the colonnades of the Court of the Women. These boxes had trumpet-shaped bronze funnels to guide donations into the box,[175] and this design amplified the sound of coins being dropped into them, indicating how much money was being donated. To choose to give in these places suggests the hypocrites were more interested in where their generosity could be heard rather than where it could be most used. In the same way, a sign that we are *giving to get* is if we prioritize our giving according to how likely it will be recognized rather than how effective it is.

Secondly: It fakes *generosity* to appear generous.

Unfortunately, giving without *kavanah* persisted within the early church.

> "Now a man named Ananias, together with his wife Sapphira, also sold a piece of property. With his wife's full knowledge he kept back part of the

money for himself, but brought the rest and put it at the apostles' feet."[176]

This couple pretended to give far more than they were giving, and so the apostle called them out on it:

"'Ananias, how is it that Satan has so filled your heart that you have lied to the Holy Spirit and have kept for yourself some of the money you received for the land?'" . . . "'What made you think of doing such a thing? You have not lied just to human beings but to God.' When Ananias heard this, he fell down and died."[177]

If you read on, you find that Ananias's wife suffered the same fate as her husband. Their sin was not what they gave but why they gave it; they were not rebuked for what was in their hands but what was in their hearts. God would have seen their sacrifice as righteous if they had simply been honest about how much they gave. Like Peter, we may be unsure what was happening in their minds, but God knew. He always does, and the Bible reminds us: "Do not be deceived; God is not mocked, for you reap whatever you sow." It is likely our hearts may not be in the right place if we deceive both ourselves and others by pretending to sacrifice more than we do.

Thirdly: It measures what's *given* rather than what's *left*.

God's thoughts are not our thoughts and He gauges our giving differently. Not only is this seen in the story of Ananias and Sapphira, but it is even more noticeable in the following example:

"As Jesus looked up, he saw the rich putting their gifts into the temple treasury. He also saw a poor widow put in two very small copper coins. 'Truly I tell you,' he said, 'this poor widow has put in more than all the others. All these people gave their gifts out of their wealth; but she out of her poverty put in all she had to live on.'"[178]

Whereas society recognizes something's value by how much we pay for it, God identifies value by how much we keep for ourselves. King David, a man after God's own heart, understood this. When he ordered a census of Israel, he committed a terrible sin because audits like this were made by rulers who wanted to bring in new taxation[179] and in the book of Deuteronomy, kings were warned not to do anything that might benefit themselves at the expense of their people.[180] So, God sent a plague that wiped out 70,000 Israelites,

severely diminishing the money David hoped to generate. David repented from his sin, and God halted the plague, so David decided to build an altar where it stopped. When the land owner told David he would give the plot for free, David replied:

> *"No, I insist on paying you for it. I will not sacrifice to the LORD my God burnt offerings that cost me nothing."* [181]

David could have seen the gift of land and oxen as God's provision, but he knew that God would focus not on what the king gave, but on what he kept back for himself. This does not mean we have to give all our wealth and possessions to God. He wants us to prosper and often uses wealth, health, and prosperity to demonstrate how He looks after His children. In fact, Jesus only suggested to one person that he should give everything he owned away.[182] This was because a rich young ruler was attempting to negotiate with Jesus. He wanted a heavenly reward with minimum earthly cost, and it tore his mind in two.

So, what principle links these stories?

They all highlight that *giving to get* is less an act of faith and more a calculated risk. This Christian-centric form of giving is an obvious hand-me-down from the old compensatory law that thinks giving a big amount will force God to do big things for us, whereas giving a small amount may only conjure up a small reward. You may have bought into it if you ask, *"What do I have to give?"*, *"How much is required?"*, or *"What guarantees will I get in return?"* You might be missing the point of giving if you waste time on trivial matters, such as whether to tithe on your gross or net income.

Sadly, if the direction of our hearts is misplaced when we give, the promise of "all these things" can become somewhat moot. Yes, God may bless us from time to time because He calls us to *test Him, and see if He will not throw open the floodgates of heaven.*[183] But, why settle for a case-by-case situation when aligning your heart will provide ongoing peace of mind?

Rewards are nice, but there are better reasons to give.

Give

Question: *When does giving attract all these things?*

Answer: *When it gives to the right things.*

With our heavenly Father, the thought matters, and He wants us to be intentional about our giving. He is not a fan of senseless service, so He is certainly not enamored with pointless giving. So, with all the opportunities, needs, and worthy causes we could put our time, finances, and talents towards, how can we know *why* to give, *how* to give, and *what* to give?

Let me answer those questions with a three-step process:

First: *Why?*

Please approach giving as an *invitation*, not a *taxation*.

Seeking *first* the Kingdom of God is an opportunity to partner with our heavenly Father. Giving is a discipline that stores up treasure in heaven, not simply for us to look forward to receiving one day, but as a war chest from which God funds His campaign to destroy the work of the evil one! If you are passionate about His campaign, you will put it first in your budget.

Second: *What?*

Please make giving *your* decision, not *God's*!

I know that may sound somewhat counter-intuitive, but please hear me out. Interestingly, when Jesus instructed us to give ourselves to pursue the Kingdom of God, He gave a principle rather than a prescription. Similarly, in the new covenant, we are not told what to give but encouraged to decide for ourselves:

> "... *give what you have decided in your heart to give, not reluctantly or under compulsion, for God loves a cheerful giver.*"[184]

In short . . . it's up to you!

Here again, Jesus begs *us* to direct *our* hearts. Yet in a church service, I am often encouraged to pray about how much I should give. But, when I do, I get the distinct impression God is wondering:

"Why on earth are you asking me?!"

God is gracious and, if needed, He will supervise us with clear instructions, as any parent would guide a little child. His aim, however, is for us to become mature and empowered to make decisions based on our greater understanding of who He is and what He wants. Although He will challenge us to give, God does not want us to feel coerced by Him. Therefore, a Kingdom-centric faith realizes that in not being prescriptive, God is inviting us to decide, "How much do you love Me?", "How often do you dream My dream?" and, importantly, "How much is My dream worth to you?"

Thirdly: How?

Please give to God what *works best*, not *feels* best.

Remember that the Biblical concept of the heart is our thoughts as well as our feelings. If you let your heart rule your head, you might be tempted to give to whatever or whoever pulls on your heartstrings the most. You might even be persuaded by a person's charisma or a sad story when God would prefer that we give to what best fulfills His plan. So, when deciding how to give, prioritize whatever will have the most significant impact because God wants us to direct our hearts, not allow our hearts to direct us!

To unpack the question I mentioned earlier.

> "Where will my giving most advance the Kingdom of God?"

You can ask the following questions as a template to guide you toward more Kingdom-centric giving:

Is it valuable?

Is this opportunity to give aligned with God's values and purpose, or is it just something I feel pressured to give to?

Is it profitable?

Is this opportunity the best way my giving can advance God's Kingdom, or is it just the first thing I can think of giving to fulfill my duty?

Is it measurable?

Can the fruit of what I give be measured to see if it works, or am I just giving to please people and feel good about myself?

Is it sustainable?

Is what I give going towards a long-lasting solution or just a temporary fix? Will it seed future work and be multiplied?

When God gave His Son, all these requirements were fulfilled!

> *"For God so loved the world, that he gave his only begotten Son, that whosoever believeth in him should not perish, but have everlasting life."*

It was valuable and fulfilled the Father's purpose of loving the world. It was not only profitable, it was the only way to redeem us from our sins. It was measured by the number of those who would believe. And it remains sustainable because it created a movement that has lasted 2,000 years!

But how does that movement grow?

Well, how much of God's work can God's people do with one hundred dollars? The answer is clear . . . One hundred dollars' worth. The advancement of God's Kingdom is an ongoing process that takes ongoing funding and that requires us to be intentional about what we give, how we give, and where we give. The good news is that when we give with *kavanah*, God anoints it, adding a supernatural boost to the work that is done with it!

In summary, Jesus gave His entire life, and He asks those He has recruited to do the same. This is not a surprise because to be a Christian is to follow His example. This offers up one final practice that we would do well to reproduce. And to help us unpack it, let me ask you this:

When Jesus did anything, what did He always do next? . . .

Recap

Our giving pivots on our motive:

- Christian-centric: *We give to get.*
- Kingdom-centric: *We get to give.*

Giving for God's purposes and our personal benefit are both Biblical, but the first is more aligned with God's heart. To seek God's Kingdom first, we will be motivated to give towards what has the greatest Kingdom impact. To raise our *kavanah*, we make ourselves aware of what God values most and give to the purpose that will best achieve it.

We start by asking: Which of the two motives drives my giving?

Reflect

Consider the following:

- Am I motivated by image rather than impact?
- Do I fake generosity to appear more generous than I am?
- Do I measure what's given rather than what's left?

Respond

Download the guide at kingdom-centric.com to:

- Approach giving as an invitation, not a taxation.
- Approach giving as your decision, not God's.
- Approach giving to what works best, not feels best.

Explore additional resources:

- Book: *Kingdom Principles: How to Develop Godly Character*
- Video: Pais Movement YouTube channel, *Kingdom-Centric Series*

10 | Discipleship

Talmidim

Capacity

I was born below average, and I finally figured out why.

In pretty much every measurement, I am naturally below par. As an infant, I was so infamously ugly that when visiting the hospital on the day of my birth, my grandmother held me up to the window to double-check what she was seeing. To my parents' chagrin, without saying another word, she returned me to the collapsible cot at the foot of my mother's bed and took a few steps toward the one adjacent to mine. Pointing to the baby she found there, my grandmother declared . . .

"Oh, this one's nice!"

I always finished last in cross-country running, could never jump over the gymnastics horse, failed horribly in art classes, and had a slight speech impediment. I was expelled from my first school at six years old for biting the girls, and when taken by my parents to my local doctor, he proclaimed:

"Mr. and Mrs. Gibbs, Paul is a problem child and always will be."

Aesthetically, academically, artistically, and athletically, I was born below average. Consequently, over the years, I have often pondered why God would choose me for what I consider to be the most important job in the world.[185] And why, in creating me with this calling in mind, He did not give me greater natural gifting. This is especially confusing when I think of so many other people I know who possess far superior inherent abilities than my own.

However, while recording a teaching video a while back, I made an unplanned comment that surprised both myself and my audience. With a dollop of hyperbole, I stated that I spend 10% of my time developing new ideas and the

remaining 90% figuring out how to help other people do what I just did.

As I said it, I suddenly realized:

I was born *below average* to help *average people* do *above-average* things!

It can be challenging for innately gifted people to pass on to others what comes naturally to them. This is because they often assume what they are gifted at will be easy for everyone else. Due to this, they may not recognize the need for any intentional or structured process. However, the advantage of being born below average is that I have been forced to develop all the skills I now have. This has helped me understand how to guide others through the process I've had to walk through. Therefore, almost anyone can learn to do what I've learned; it simply requires practice and a little self-discipline.

My weaknesses have become my strengths!

I love seeing the same practices and principles God taught me reproduced in others—often to a greater degree. Of course, I am still responsible for developing my skills, but each time I improve in an area, I can also help others improve similarly. It's an incredible feeling to help someone unlock their divine potential for Kingdom advancement!

It's like being a superhero! . . . Without having superpowers . . . or being a hero.

But what about you?

> *"Therefore go and make disciples of all nations, baptizing them in the name of the Father and of the Son and of the Holy Spirit, and teaching them to obey everything I have commanded you."*[186]

Jesus came to change the world by bringing heaven to earth, and the best way He knew how to do this was through discipleship. So in whatever Jesus did, what He *always did next* was disciple others to do the same! And then, He said, "Tag, you're it!"

Which leads me to ask: Who are you discipling?

Just as all healthy things reproduce, disciples should produce more disciples. The Father expects that what He has invested in you will be multiplied, and the great news is that every one of us can do it!

The bad news is that we may not know what 'it' actually is.

It

Scholars estimate that there are only 8,000 to 9,000 different Hebrew words in the Old Testament. Compare that to the 1,022,000 words in the English language, of which 171,476 are commonly used today.[187] Therefore, some Hebrew words can be broad and generic relative to the precise English translation. A portion of them can contain various meanings and nuances that only become clear if we know the context in which they are spoken.

This is undoubtedly true with the Hebrew term for disciple:

> *Talmid:* Disciple. Apprentice. Student. Learner.[188]

As you will see, this disparity between languages has limited our understanding of the method Jesus believed would lead to the Kingdom's coming. During the Second Temple period in which He recruited His disciples, there were two stages to following a rabbi. Although the disciples went through both, this is not seen clearly in the English translation of our Bibles. Plus, our Christian-centric religion focuses almost entirely on the first stage, rarely equipping us to progress to the second. Yet this second stage is the catalyst to advancing God's Kingdom!

So, what was the two-step process?

According to the historian Ray Vander Laan, a rabbi had two types of followers:

Students and *disciples*.

A student would seek out a rabbi, listen to their teaching, and decide which instructions they wished to apply to their lives. A disciple, however, would join a rabbi on his journey, learning to copy his actions in order to become like him.

> A student wanted to *know* what the rabbi *knew*.
>
> But a disciple wanted to *do* what the rabbi *did*.

Often, one stage led to another, as we see played out with the twelve disciples:

> *"Jesus went out to a mountainside to pray, and spent the night praying to God. When morning came, he called his disciples to him and chose twelve of them, whom he also designated apostles . . ."*[189]

Although our English translation uses different words, the process is clear; the twelve were chosen from a larger group of students and became Jesus' disciples. They leaped from merely believing in Jesus' words to learning first-hand how to do what He did.

The two stages of discipleship are also mirrored in the two Christianities.

To be Christian-centric is to study what Jesus did to pursue a godly life and reap its benefits. To be Kingdom-centric is to go beyond that. Driven by a desire to give God what He wants, it is to advance God's Kingdom, God's way, by making more disciples.

Therefore, our discipleship pivots on how we follow God:

> Christian-centric: As *students of* Jesus.

> Kingdom-centric: As *disciplers for* Jesus.

And so, here is my tenth awkward question for you:

> Which of the two types of follower are you?

Do you study the words of Jesus to apply them to your life? Or to also train others to do the same? Is your goal for discipleship simply to become 'closer' to the Father, or is it also to bring others closer to Him? To raise our *kavanah*, we must spend time in His presence, noticing His Kingdom principles and practices, in order to demonstrate and pass them on to others. This way, we will multiply what God has done in us by recruiting others to do the same.

Before we look at how any follower of Jesus, young or old, male or female, experienced or inexperienced, can fulfill His command, let's first ask: Why might we remain at step one?

Student

Question: *When is discipleship, not discipleship?*

Answer: *When it is all about the disciple.*

In Christian-centric Christianity, a fundamentally individualistic religion, discipleship focuses almost entirely on shaping individual Christians to know God better. This has created a culture that has made discipling others an optional upgrade for those particularly excited about their faith. However, if you think that the sole purpose of discipleship is *your* journey toward God, you have missed the point of God's ultimate plan. Everything God does in us should flow through us into the lives of others.

In the companion book, *The Kingdom Centric Church*, I suggest how leaders can create a discipleship culture. After all, a Christian-centric church will never produce Kingdom-centric Christians. In this chapter, however, let me highlight why most followers of Jesus are not fulfilling one of Jesus' most important commands.

Recently, the Barna Group surveyed committed Christians to ask why so few are intentionally discipling anyone else. The top three answers they gave are incredibly insightful,[190] and most are based on common misconceptions. I will share them in reverse order, and as I do, can I encourage you to take a look to see if you relate to any of them?

In Third Place: *"I just haven't thought about it."*

But then, why would you?

Unsurprisingly, if the Gospel you heard was 'Jesus came to rescue you,' rather than 'Jesus came to recruit you,' discipling others will appear to be an added feature. You might even have demoted it to the category of a ministry gift. I've actually heard people say, "I'm not gifted to disciple people," and "Discipleship is not my calling."

But discipleship is not a gift; it's why we are given gifts in the first place!

Adding to this misconception is that many Christians feel arrogant even to consider discipling others. The zeitgeist of our modern Western world implies that presenting ourselves as knowing more than others is somehow wrong. If the world, rather than the Word, determines your thinking, you may be left believing that only a chosen few can be disciplers. I would like to demolish that notion for you. Please realize that all Christians can, and should, willingly embrace both parts of discipleship—being discipled *and* discipling others. In fact, as you will see, discipleship is perhaps one of the most humble acts

a follower of Jesus can perform because it makes everything you do, less about you, and more about others!

In Second Place: *"No one has suggested it or asked me."*

Please don't let that stop you!

Religion has always created a kind of 'them and us' dynamic. Traditionally, Christianity has emphasized clergy and laity, often using formal Christian education as a dividing line. However, Jesus discounted this when choosing His disciples, even reminding them:

> *"You did not choose me, but I chose you . . ."*[191]

Taking a little time to understand why Jesus said this may encourage you to be a discipler for Him. So, let me provide some context and explain how students became disciplers.[192]

> Step 1: At six years old, children were taught the Torah, the first five books of the Bible, and they would memorize it. This first level of education was called *Bet Sefer*, which means 'House of the Book.'

> Step 2: At ten years old, only the top students would enter *Bet Talmud*, the 'House of Learning.' Those who made it would begin to memorize the rest of the Old Testament's Tanakh at this level. They would be expected to learn what various commentators had taught about these scriptures and where their authority had come from to teach what they taught. Those who were not accepted would return home, often to join the family business.

> Step 3: The best students would apply to become a *talmid* after age fourteen. This level is called *Bet Midrash*, which means 'House of Study.' These students would seek a position as a disciple by approaching a rabbi and asking if they could follow him. If yes, they would become part of the rabbi's entourage or *talmidim*.[193]

But the disciples did not approach Jesus; He approached them . . .

Why?

Because Jesus was looking for something in His disciples that the usual

process did not seem to provide. When a student approached a rabbi, he would be accepted if he was a good academic candidate. To fulfill the primary ability that most rabbis were looking for they would ask:

"Will this child be able to pass on my 'yoke'?"

A yoke was the compilation of things a rabbi would "bind" (forbid) or "loosen" (permit), and a disciple's primary role was to pass on this teaching to others. Essentially, they were chosen based on their ability to memorize and regurgitate what the rabbi said. By reminding the disciples that He chose them, Jesus was pointing out that He wanted something more from them than mere academia, telling them He had:

". . . appointed you so that you might go and bear fruit . . ." [194]

There is that word again . . . fruit.

Jesus believed ordinary people could disciple others if they were willing to serve Him and show others how to do the same. He was looking for the exact opposite of what He saw in the religious leaders of the time:

"The teachers of the law and the Pharisees sit in Moses' seat. So you must be careful to do everything they tell you. But do not do what they do, for they do not practice what they preach." [195]

He uses the phrase *'sit in Moses' seat'* to highlight that these religious leaders had the authority and qualifications to teach God's law,[196] but He points out that although they were good talkers, they were not good doers. And this is hugely important, because Jesus understood that people will do what they see us do, not what they hear us say!

Sure, no one may have suggested you make disciples, but with the possible exception of those who previously had been John's disciples, no one had suggested it to the twelve either! But when Jesus called them, they responded. So now that Jesus has called you, will you do the same?

In First Place: *"I don't think I'm qualified or equipped."*

Well, okay, that's probably true. But then again, neither was I when I started discipling people. This may be because most church leaders don't feel equipped themselves as very few of us were discipled in how to make disciplers.

It's a case of the blind leading the blind.

It is important to note that discipleship is more than simply education. Words are cheap. They are easy to listen to and easy to pass on. The Swiss theologian Karl Barth has often been attributed with saying:

> "The Word became flesh, and then through theologians, it became words again."

This was the problem I had many years ago when I was asked not to train young people on the job, but instead to bring them back into a classroom setting. The operating system I had become part of clashed with the methodology of Jesus that I was attempting to replicate.

It drove me to ask:

> "Why is it that when Jesus took people on an experience that led to education, we educate people and hope they have an experience?"

The biggest problem I have when training people to disciple others is our default instinct to simply teach people rather than taking them on our journey and providing them with an example. Discipleship is more than teaching others what you know; it is training them to do what you do. Unfortunately, telling people what to do is much easier than showing them, especially if no one has shown you . . . or you're not doing it yourself.

Many of our church leaders were educated in a Bible college. They sat in classes that taught them how to educate students but were not given the experience that showed them how to help disciples become disciplers. It's no one's fault; it's just how it is, but that cycle must be broken. A new movement has to start somewhere; perhaps it can start with you. If so, what qualifies you to disciple others?

Well, less than you might think.

Disciplers

Question: *When is discipleship true discipleship?*

Answer: *When it is limited.*

Discipleship, done right, requires less time than you might think. Since starting to disciple people, I have had two children and three grandchildren, started an organization and a business, led a few churches, written multiple books, and generally had a lot of fun. That's because I have not had to create opportunities to disciple people; I have just had to include them in what I am already doing! This does, however, require higher levels of *kavanah* because I must have enough *intention* in what I do to invite others on my journey and make a little space to educate them as we go.

You can develop your discipleship ability by reading or watching my practical teaching, *Talmidim: How to Disciple Anyone in Anything*,[197] but all you need to get started is to ask three simple questions:

What am I doing to advance God's Kingdom?

How have I learned to do it?

Who can I take with me?

If we all as Christians embrace our *'What,' 'How,'* and *'Who,'* and churches intentionally equip us to do it, we will change the world!

First: *What's your 'what'?*

"Therefore go . . ."[198]

The problem is, go where? You can go to many places, but you cannot go everywhere or do everything. I would advise asking:

"What am I already doing that most advances God's Kingdom?"

Maybe it is connected to your passion or driven by a complaint. My complaint was that our local churches were not reaching the teenagers who desperately needed to hear the Gospel. Perhaps your 'what' is intercessory prayer, hospitality, organization, comforting, or some other current act of service?

Once you have that in mind, there are some misconceptions to free yourself from, so let me offer the following advice:

There's no need to disciple anyone in everything.

Jesus didn't.

One common misconception is that only very mature Christians can disciple other people. And that might be true if you aspire to become some kind of spiritual guru. However, you only need to be one step ahead of those you're discipling in your 'what.' Jesus, for example, focused His discipleship on what He was already doing: the work of an apostle, preaching, healing, praying, and making more disciples. He didn't train the twelve in every aspect of life or scripture. Instead, He left many things for the Holy Spirit to teach them at a later date.[199]

There's no need to disciple anyone forever.

Jesus trained His twelve disciples for three years; that's how long it took to get them ready. You might only need to do it for three weeks. Alternatively, I've been discipling some people for twenty years. Essentially, disciple someone until they can do whatever you are showing them to do, without you.

There's no need to disciple everyone to the same extent.

Jesus had different levels of intentional relationship with those He taught. This truth has even been noted among the twelve apostles. You also don't have to disciple people individually. You can do it as a group, which takes less time and is more effective as those you disciple start learning from each other.

It's important to note that you don't need to create anything new to disciple someone. Just include them in the most effective thing you are already doing! In fact, some scholars argue that a more accurate translation of the Greek word translated as 'go' is "as you go." Technically correct or not, it certainly better describes how discipleship is best accomplished: as you do what you are already doing, make disciples!

Of course, if you are not doing anything to advance the Kingdom of God, you might need to figure that out first. Perhaps as you use this book to become more Kingdom-centric, one idea might be to invite others to join you in that process. Whatever you decide your 'what' is, don't wait long until you invite others into your journey!

Second: *What's your 'how'?*

> *". . . Teaching them to obey everything I have commanded you."*[200]

Once you recognize your 'what,' make a note of your 'how'—the practices and spiritual principles God has taught you as you learned to do what you do. Don't presume other people know these things. Take time to write them down and order them so that someone else can understand them.

Ask yourself:

> How do I practically do what I do?
>
> What are the principles of the Kingdom I have learned along the way?
>
> How can I record these principles and practices so I can pass them on?

When you have thought these things through and put them in order, that is good enough to start. Again: "To teach is to learn twice!" Discipling others will help you refine what you teach people over time, and journeying together will highlight gaps you can address in your own understanding. Even mistakes will help you improve on what you are already doing!

Third: *Who's your 'who'?*

> *". . . and make disciples of all nations . . ."*[201]

Don't play God.

Don't look for disciples by choosing in advance who you think will be interested. You may limit the options because you consciously or subconsciously reject certain people, thinking, "Oh, they won't be interested" or "I'm not interested in them." Just keep your mind open to possibilities. I have even had the opportunity to disciple those not yet Christians because they were leaning forward and interested in doing what I do. Teaching them my 'how' allowed me to share my faith with them. So, offer yourself to anyone by sharing what you do and what God has taught you. Do this in any appropriate setting and, if possible, ask your leaders to give you opportunities. Don't be dismayed if no one initially responds; keep offering, and someone eventually will.

There are, however, some caveats, and here are my tips for ensuring that those who do respond are people you should disciple:

They must be willing and able to participate in what you do.

You must believe that they can go on to do what you do.

You must believe that they are willing to commit to the process.

I encourage you to meet with whomever you decide to disciple in order to set your expectations of them, such as how often they need to join you in whatever you are doing, and what they might need to prepare in advance. Although this may sound a little formal, it's worth doing to give God what He wants!

What started when I became a Christian at 13 may have led nowhere if the young men willing to rent a tent had not provided a way for me to receive discipleship. I doubt they knew that by training a below-average schoolboy, they would indirectly reach millions more around the world. But that's the beauty of discipleship; it makes it less about what we do and more about what He can do with it. In 1988, school outreach was my 'what.' I focused on improving my communication skills and regularly visited 17 schools, connecting with 10,000 students yearly. I gradually learned 'how' to do it well. However, as one person, I had minimal impact. So, in 1992, Lynn and I began to look for 'who' we could disciple to do what we did. Fast forward 30 years, and the number of those reached by those who have been discipled is beyond counting, and the teenagers we have integrated into faith communities have multiplied exponentially.

Yet this became a reality because, when I first shared the vision, my pastor equipped me to do the work God had called me to do.

Now I'm all about discipleship, and I hope how I have written this book highlights that. If you are not a preacher, you may not notice that I have set every chapter out in a particular order: An introduction to the subject, an explanation of the pivot, then three points to avoid being Christian-centric, and three to become more Kingdom-centric (preachers love three points). In this way, I hope to make it easy for every Christian leader to not only absorb it themselves but go on to share what I have written.

Why?

Because discipleship helps us make everything less about *our ministry* and

more about building a culture to advance *His mission*.

So, if this book has inspired and helped you, I pray that you will not only go on the journey to become more Kingdom-centric, but overtake me and offer new insights!

In summary, imagine if all of us were discipled to make disciples. The Kingdom would grow within us and through us—and the world would become a very different place! God would be glorified and, most importantly, He would receive what He wants. But that will only happen when we as followers run with the dreams and visions He puts in our hearts, and when our leaders equip us for works of service prepared in advance for us to do!

This motivates me to begin a further awkward conversation . . . One that requires another book . . . One that asks the question:

What might a Kingdom-centric church look like? . . .

Recap

Our discipleship pivots on how we follow:

- Christian-centric: As *students of* Jesus.
- Kingdom-centric: As *disciplers for* Jesus.

To become more Kingdom-centric, we advance God's Kingdom, God's way, by making more disciples. The goal for our discipleship is not only to advance the Kingdom of God more successfully in and through us but also to train others to do the same. Therefore, we raise our *kavanah* by demonstrating what God has taught us and then passing on to others the principles and practices we have learned.

We start by asking: Which of the two types of follower am I?

Reflect

Consider the following:

- Have I thought about discipling others?
- Am I waiting for someone to suggest or ask me?
- Do I think I'm neither qualified nor equipped?

Respond

Download the guide at kingdom-centric.com to:

- Discover your 'what'.
- Make note of your 'how'.
- Recruit your 'who'.

Explore additional resources:

- Book: *Talmidim: How to Disciple Anyone in Anything*
- Video: Pais Movement YouTube channel, *Kingdom-Centric Series*
- See Next Steps for Leaders on the following pages..

Thank you for taking the time to read this book. If you have found the content helpful and thought-provoking, please leave a review on GoodReads, Amazon, or your platform of choice to encourage others toward becoming more Kingdom-centric. Together, we can Reframe Christianity. God bless you!

Next Steps for Leaders.

The Kingdom-Centric Masterclass.

Book a Masterclass for your training event, conference, retreat, or amalgamate it with a church Sunday service. The Masterclass is an interactive training event providing creative templates, Biblical knowledge, and practical application in a fun learning environment.

The program consists of two complementary courses designed to reframe both individuals and church structures:

- **Participants gain:** An understanding of God's Kingdom. A knowledge of Kingdom principles and practices. A vision for their role in God's Kingdom.
- **Content includes:** A digital tool to assess a Kingdom-centric mindset. A Biblical perspective of the Kingdom. A challenge to seek first the Kingdom of God.

Access our user-friendly online platform for easy appraisal. Benefit from comprehensive slides, notes, videos, and consultancy sessions tailored to your needs.

The Kingdom-Centric Project.

Is your church ready to embark on a transformative journey towards becoming truly Kingdom-centric? Empower your congregation through our comprehensive program tailored for both congregations and leaders. Engage in practical workshops and consultancy sessions. Benefit from continued support and guidance as you journey towards Kingdom-centricity.

The program consists of two complementary courses designed to reframe both individuals and church structures:

- **Congregation:** Engage in a series of 10 transformative topics covering crucial aspects like Gospel, Prayer, Discipleship, and more.
- **Leaders:** Dive deep into 10 essential templates for building a Kingdom-centric church, facilitated through workshops and consultancy sessions.

Access our user-friendly online platform for easy appraisal. Benefit from comprehensive slides, notes, videos, and consultancy sessions tailored to your needs.

Endnotes

1. Matthew 6:33
2. Stausberg, Michael, and Mark Q. Gardiner, eds, "Definition", in *The Oxford Handbook of the Study of Religion* (Oxford: Oxford University Press, 2017), 9-32.
3. Matthew 23
4. Matthew 5:17
5. Philippians 2:12b-13
6. John 4:23
7. John 14:6
8. John 3:16
9. Matthew 6:31-33
10. I unpack this in the book *Kingdom Principles: Developing Godly Character*
11. For more details of how pagans would consult an oracle read *The Kingdom Principles: Developing Godly Character*
12. Philippians 2:21
13. John 15:7
14. 1 Timothy 2:3-4
15. Strong's H8666. NB: *teshuvot* is the plural of *teshuva*. The word is also used to indicate an answer or to answer.
16. Lamentations 5:21 CJB
17. Matthew 12:43-45 (The Message Translation; a paraphrase of the Bible in contemporary English).
18. Rochel Chein studied in Jerusalem and lives in New York where she writes for Chabad.org.
19. An example of this connection is made in Kiddushin 66b where the Jewish Gemara comments on Numbers 25:12.
20. Cornelius Plantinga, *Not the Way It's Supposed to Be* (Grand Rapids, MI: Eerdmans, 1999), 10.
21. Isaiah 14:12-15
22. Strong's G758 - archōn.
23. 1 John 3:8b
24. John 12:31

ENDNOTES

25. Luke 10:9; 17:20-2.

26. Luke 17:20-2. Matthew 12:28; 25:34.

27. Luke 22:18. Matthew 6:9-10; 25:31-34.

28. Matthew 6:33 (NLT, 1996).

29. Luke 10:8-9

30. Matthew 13:1-23

31. Gamaliel the Elder was a prominent Jewish rabbi and teacher referenced in Acts who is thought to have been born in 10 BC.

32. Philo of Alexandria lived somewhere between 20 BC and 50 AD. He was a Jewish philosopher who lived in Alexandria, Egypt.

33. In the first year of our marriage, we moved to Harpurhey, UK, and then next door to Moston where these incidents took place. To understand more read Manchester Evening News. "Harpurhey, the worst place in England." February 19, 2007. https://www.manchestereveningnews.co.uk/news/greater-manchester-news/harpurhey-the-worst-place-in-england-1108111?utm_source=linkCopy&utm_medium=social&utm_campaign=sharebar.

34. Wikipedia Contributors. "Murder of Suzanne Capper." Wikipedia, last modified January 23, 2024, https://en.wikipedia.org/wiki/Murder_of_Suzanne_Capper.

35. Manchester Evening News. "Harpurhey, the worst place in England." February 19, 2007. https://www.manchestereveningnews.co.uk/news/greater-manchester-news/harpurhey-the-worst-place-in-england-1108111?utm_source=linkCopy&utm_medium=social&utm_campaign=sharebar.

36. Matthew 12:45 (The Message Translation; a paraphrase of the Bible in contemporary English).

37. Matthew 6:33 (emphasis mine)

38. The Hacienda was a nightclub in Manchester, UK, and its story is told in the book *The Hacienda: How Not to Run a Club* by Peter Hook.

39. David Flusser and Steven Notley. *The Sage from Galilee: Rediscovering Jesus' Genius*, 4th ed. (Grand Rapids, MI: Eerdmans, 2007). .

40. Job 4:7: "Consider now: who, being innocent, has ever perished? Where were the upright ever destroyed?"

41. Psalms 73:12-14. Jeremiah 12:1. Habakkuk 1:13. Malachi 3:15.

42. Strong's G1343

43. NB: I downloaded an audio copy of Rabbi Dovid Bendory's "Speaking with God" teaching series, but the website with this resource has since been deleted.

44. As the common language of Jesus' day was Aramaic, it is important to note that the specific phrasing of the question has evolved since; however, the question of *kavanah* was certainly present in the Jewish tradition of His day.

45. Pinchas Giller. *Shalom Shar'abi and the Kabbalists of Beit El*, 1st ed. (Oxford: Oxford University Press, 2008), 20.

46. Luke 22:19-20

47. Rabbi Dovid Bendory taught this on his podcast, which has since been deleted.

48. 1 Samuel 13:14. Acts 13:22.

49. 2 Samuel 11-12

50. Psalms 51:10-12

51. It's interesting to note that the Hebrew word for 'anointed,' *Mâshîyach* (Strong's H4899), connects anointing to someone consecrated and brought in line with God's purposes. Used 39 times, often in conjunction with the Messiah, the word directly refers to Him twice.

52. 1 John 5:14

53. James 5:16b

54. Mark 7:9-13 (Text altered from the NIV Corban to the more common Jewish spelling *korban*)

55. Strong's G2878

56. Such as giving food offerings to God during a festival when they themselves would consume it.

57. Rabbi Eliyahu Dessler. Michtav Me'Eliyahu (New York, NY: Feldheim Publishers, 2004) 3:66.

58. 1 Corinthians 10:23

59. This was also due to their misinterpretation of scriptures such as Malachi 3:1-4 - "But who can endure the day of his coming? Who can stand when he appears? For he will be like a refiner's fire or a launderer's soap. He will sit as a refiner and purifier of silver; he will purify the Levites and refine them like gold and silver."

60. Matthew 15:8-9

61. Matthew 23:25-28

62. Matthew 23:2-3a

63. Matthew 23:3b-4

64. Philippians 2:12c-13

65. Matthew 5:27-28

66. Hebrews 5:12-13

67. Hebrews 5:14

68. John 1:1

69. Molly McBride Jacobson. "Robert the Bruce's Heart." Atlas Obscura, February 16, 2017, https://www.atlasobscura.com/places/robert-the-bruces-heart.

70. He was represented in a pillar of cloud leading the Israelites. His presence in a cloud threw their enemies into confusion. He appeared in glory in a cloud. He spoke to Moses in a dense cloud. His presence appeared as a cloud above the tabernacle. He enveloped the people as a cloud at Jesus' baptism. He will arrive on a cloud in the second coming. He will sit on a cloud at the time of judgment. Exodus 13:21; Exodus 14:24; Exodus 16:10; Exodus 19:9; Numbers 9:15; Matthew 17:5; Matthew 24:30; Revelation 14:14.

71. Hebrews 5:11

72. Hebrews 5:14.

73. 2 Timothy 3:16

74. Matthew 5:29

75. Matthew 5:30

76. Attributed to William Carey through multiple sources. Carey was an English Christian missionary who founded the Serampore College and the Serampore University. He is seen as the father of modern missions.

77. John 14:6

78. Hebrews 5:12

79. Strong's G4747

80. The book, *Haverim: How to Study Anything with Anyone* by Paul Clayton Gibbs, is available at Amazon.com and other bookstores. The template and more resources can be found at HaverimDevotions.com.

81. Hebrews 10:24-25b

82. Strong's G1485

83. Justin Nortey and Michael Rotolo. "How the Pandemic Has Affected Attendance at U.S. Religious Services." Pew Research Center, March 28, 2023. https://www.pewresearch.org/religion/2023/03/28/how-the-pandemic-has-affected-attendance-at-u-s-religious-services/#:~:text=One%2Din%2Dfive%20U.S.%20adults,often%20than%20before%20COVID%2D19.

84. Why Millennials Aren't Watching Your Streamed Worship Services," Barna Group, October 5, 2022, https://www.barna.com/research/millennials-arent-watching/.

85. Strong's G3948

86. Acts 15:39a

87. John 13:35

88. 1 John 4:20

89. Matthew 25:37-40

90. James 1:27

91. Matthew 6:14-15

92. Colossians 1:24b

93. 1 Corinthians 14:26

94. Prince William attended from 2001 to 2005 and earned a degree in Geography whilst living in St. Salvator's Hall. Prince William's wife, Catherine Middleton, also attended, and the two of them met while they were students there. Others include Princess Eugenie and Zara Tindall.

95. Colossians 3:16

96. Earl Jabay, Kingdom of Self, 1st ed. (Lancaster, PA: Logos Associates, 1980).

97. Ephesians 5:19

98. 1 Corinthians 15:42-44. 2 Corinthians 5:1-4. Philippians 3:20-21.

99. 1 Corinthians 2:9. John 14:2-3.

100. Psalm 67:1-2. Genesis 12:2-3.

101. Matthew 17:20

102. James 5:16b

103. Luke 11:1b

104. Luke 11:1c

105. Many books unpack the *Amidah*, but an overview can be found on Wikipedia.

106. Matthew 6:10. NB: In Luke we are told the reason Jesus gave the disciples this prayer, and in Matthew it records the full version. It is possible Jesus shared this prayer on separate occasions with variations.

107. David Bivin and Roy Blizzard Jr., *Understanding the Difficult Words of Jesus: New Insights From a Hebrew Perspective* (Shippensburg, PA: Destiny Image Publishers, 2001), 77. David Bivin was the co-founder of The Jerusalem Perspective and the founder of the Jerusalem School of Synoptic Research.

108. Matthew 9:38

109. Liana Miate, "Fates," World History Encyclopedia, December 16, 2022, www.worldhistory.org/Fates/#google_vignette.

110. Romans 10:17

111. Hebrews 11:6

112. The Norns are female entities in Norse mythology that play a significant role in determining the destiny and fate of both gods and mortals. They are often described as weavers of fate. See www.britannica.com/topic/Norn for more.

113. The Bokmål Dictionary referenced in Wikipedia's commentary on its Old Norse etymology.

ENDNOTES

114. Proverbs 13:12a

115. Proverbs 4:23

116. John Kass, "'Walk on Water' Plan Is Too True to Be Ignored," Chicago Tribune, last updated August 10, 2021, https://www.chicagotribune.com/1999/02/08/walk-on-water-plan-is-too-true-to-be-ignored/.

117. 2 Timothy 4:3-4

118. Ephesians 6:12 (MEV)

119. 1 John 5:14-15

120. Genesis 15:6

121. Romans 2:2

122. It was first discovered and documented in the late 19th century by neuroscientists such as Santiago Ramón y Cajal and William James. Ramón y Cajal's work in the late 19th and early 20th centuries contributed to our understanding. Eric Kandel, James Schwartz, and Thomas Jessell, *Principles of Neural Science*, 4th ed. (New York, NY: McGraw Hill Medical, 2000).

123. Philippians 3:17

124. Strong's G5179

125. Matthew 6:10

126. Reports from *The Sun* newspaper and *The London Evening Standard* newspaper are shown in a documentary clip found on YouTube. You can watch the miracle on YouTube by searching 'Jean Neil Healing.'

127. Mark 8:12

128. Joel 2:28-29

129. Matthew 4:19

130. Jonah 3:1-2

131. Exodus 3:7-8

132. Genesis 12:1-2

133. *Lekh lekha* are the fifth and sixth words in the *parashah* that cover Genesis 12:1–17:27. A "Parashat" is a weekly reading from the Torah and with other "*parashot*", they ensure that the entire Torah is covered over the course of a year.

134. Keren Pryor, *A Taste of Torah* (Marshfield, MO: First Fruits of Zion, 2016). Also see Batya Ellinoy. "Go Forth." Jewish Boston, November 6, 2019, https://www.jewishboston.com/read/go-forth/.

135. Genesis 17:4-5

136. Acts 9:3b-4

137. According to the Barna Group, only 6% of Christians accepted Jesus after age 18, and the International Bible Society stated 83% converted between ages 4 and 14.

138. Matthew 26:39

139. 2 Corinthians 11:23b-25

140. Matthew 5:41

141. Some of his most notable books include *The Pursuit of God*, *The Knowledge of the Holy*, and *The Attributes of God*.

142. A.W. Tozer, *The Knowledge of the Holy* (New York: HarperCollins Publishers, 1978), 1.

143. 1 Corinthians 1:27a

144. John 1:42

145. Exodus 3:2

146. Exodus 3:9-10

147. Exodus 32:31-32

148. Ecclesiastes 3:11b-c

149. Proverbs 13:12a

150. "The Future of World Religions: Population Growth Projections 2010-2050," Pew Research Center, April 2, 2015, https://www.pewresearch.org/religion/2015/04/02/religious-projections-2010-2050/.

151. 2 Corinthians 4:4

152. Matthew 16:18b

153. 2 Timothy 4:2

154. Existential philosophers like Jean-Paul Sartre and Martin Heidegger emphasized the idea that humans should focus on being rather than doing. Buddhist teachings encourage individuals to cultivate a state of being rather than being consumed by constant activity. Transcendentalist thinkers like Ralph Waldo Emerson and Henry David Thoreau promoted similar ideas.

155. Ephesians 2:10

156. Strong's G2041

157. Luke 3:8. Matthew 25:14-30. Proverbs 13:4. Psalm 1:1-3.

158. Matthew 21:43

159. The author is not referring to the modern hasidic movement but the people that predate them and Jesus' time on earth.

ENDNOTES

160. Lois Tverberg, *Walking in the Dust of Rabbi Jesus: How the Jewish Words of Jesus Can Change Your Life* (Grand Rapids, MI: Zondervan, 2012).

161. Mark 9:38-41

162. Matthew 5:46-48

163. Matthew 6:33

164. This material is contained in both a book that can be found on amazon.com and a video series found at the website mypais.com.

165. Matthew 6:25a

166. Strong's G3309. Derived from the root word *meris* (μέρις), meaning "a part" or "a share," and conveys the idea of being divided or distracted in one's thoughts or cares.

167. The concept of cognitive dissonance was introduced by Festinger in his 1957 book titled *A Theory of Cognitive Dissonance*. This seminal work outlines the theory and explores the psychological discomfort that arises when a person holds two or more contradictory beliefs, values, or attitudes simultaneously.

168. Matthew 6:24

169. United States Declaration of Independence. Adopted by the Continental Congress on July 4, 1776.

170. Nehemiah 8:10

171. James 1:8

172. Psalm 51:12

173. Philippians 4:11b

174. Matthew 6:2

175. Leen Ritmeyer, "The Treasury of the Temple in Jerusalem," Ritmeyer Archaeological Design, last updated May 15, 2015, https://www.ritmeyer.com/2015/05/15/the-treasury-of-the-temple-in-jerusalem/.

176. Acts 5:1-2

177. Acts 5:3, 4b-5a

178. Luke 21:1-4

179. Exodus 30:11-16. 2 Chronicles 24:6-9.

180. Deuteronomy 17:17

181. 2 Samuel 24:24

182. Matthew 19:16-22

183. Based on Malachi 3:10.

184. 2 Corinthians 9:7

185. Founder and Global Director of the Pais Movement. www.pais.life.

186. Matthew 28:19-20a

187. The current number according to the Oxford English Dictionary. Note that this number grows constantly.

188. An amalgamation of the article "Rabbi and Talmidim" by Ray Vander Laan found at the website ThatTheWorldMayKnow.com. Also reference Strong's H8527.

189. Luke 6:12-13

190. 'U.S. Christians on barriers to making disciples.' U.S. Christian adults who are not disciple-makers, December 22, 2020-January 18, 202. Barna Group 2022

191. John 15:16a

192. NB: I came across various versions of this process in my studies regarding the Second Temple period. Ultimately, although terms may be interchanged amongst them, they all lead to the same conclusion. I have therefore outlined a composite of what I discovered reflecting the most common descriptions on the subject.

193. *Talmidim* is the plural of *talmid*.

194. John 15:16a

195. Matthew 23:2-3

196. In Jewish tradition, the teachers of the law would occupy a position of authority similar to that of Moses, who received the Law from God and delivered it to the people of Israel. By saying that the teachers of the law sit in Moses' seat, Jesus acknowledged their official position as interpreters of the Law.

197. This material is contained in both a book that can be found on amazon.com and a video series found at the website mypais.com.

198. Matthew 28:19a

199. John 14:26: "But the Advocate, the Holy Spirit, whom the Father will send in my name, will teach you all things and will remind you of everything I have said to you."

200. Matthew 28:20a

201. Matthew 28:19a

pais™

Together with his wife, Lynn, Paul Clayton Gibbs pioneered the Pais Movement. 30+ years on, Pais offers three programs that invite you to a life on mission. Pais equips Christians to advance the Kingdom of God with new concepts, tools, and templates.

Apprenticeship
Be discipled and make disciples
Join a team. Go on mission!

Academy
Mobilize your youth.
Use our program!

Allies
Equip Your Church.
Empower Your People.

visit pais.life for more info

About the Author

Paul Clayton Gibbs is the creator of The Shapes Test and the KingdomCentric assessment. He and his wife, The Foxy Lynn, have two adult sons and are the proud grandparents of two beautiful girls and a handsome boy. Originally from Manchester, England, the Gibbs family moved to the USA in 2005.

As founder of The Pais Movement, a faith-based organization that creates workable symmetry between organizations, Paul seeks to help people raise their *kavanah* when it comes to living out a missional lifestyle to advance God's Kingdom. Paul has written several books and spends a significant amount of time traveling throughout the world speaking at conferences, businesses, churches and other acting as a consultant for various networks. His primary topics are leadership development, mentoring, and missional living. He is the CEO of Masterclass Suites, LLC, and is also the creator of various training 'templates' aimed at 'Mobilizing the many, not just the few.'

Paul enjoys swimming, sailing, bodyboarding, skiing, snowboarding, mountain biking and is a lifelong Manchester United fan!

instagram paulcgibbs
facebook paulclaytongibbs